DISCOVERING
DISNEYLAND PARIS

Tips and Tricks for Beginners

Asaf Iqbal

Amazon Publishing

To Gillian, my beloved wife and the ultimate Disney enthusiast,

This book is a testament to your unwavering love for all things Disney and the magic it brings into our lives. From the enchanting tales to the unforgettable characters, you have shown me the power of imagination and the joy it can spark.

Your passion for Disney has fuelled my own fascination with Disneyland Paris and inspired me to embark on this journey of discovery. Through the ups and downs of creating this book, your unwavering support, encouragement, and endless enthusiasm have been my guiding light.

May this book serve as a tribute to the countless hours of joy and laughter we have shared within the walls of Disneyland Paris. From our magical adventures together to the dreams we continue to chase, I dedicate these pages to you, my partner-in-crime and fellow dreamer.

Thank you for being the Minnie to my Mickey , the Wendy to my Peter, and the eternal source of magic in my life. This book is as much yours as it is mine, for without your love and Disney spirit, it would not have come to be.

With all my love,
Asaf

FOREWORD

As an ardent Disneyland Paris enthusiast, I am thrilled to extend my warmest welcome to you. Within the pages of this book, I am delighted to share my passion, expertise, and insider knowledge gathered from numerous visits to the parks over the past 14 months.

Whether adventuring as a couple or with my own family, I have immersed myself in the magical wonders of Disneyland Paris, unearthing hidden gems and uncovering the secrets that make each visit truly extraordinary.

With the privilege of our annual infinity passes, my family and I have acquired invaluable wisdom and firsthand experiences that can enhance your own journey. From navigating the intricacies of the parks to discovering the best dining options and finding remarkable deals on food and souvenirs, Together, let us embark on an enchanting voyage of exploration through the captivating world of Disneyland Paris.

Join me as we unravel the secrets, unlock the joys, and create memories that will last a lifetime.

INTRODUCTION

Imagine stepping through the gates of a magical kingdom, where dreams come true and happiness knows no bounds. The air is filled with excitement and anticipation as families and friends gather, eager to embark on a once-in-a-lifetime adventure. The sight of towering castles, vibrant parades, and beloved characters brings smiles to the faces of both young and old. Welcome to Disneyland Paris, a place where imagination knows no limits and where cherished memories are made.

Whether you are a seasoned traveler or embarking on your very first journey, Discovering Disneyland Paris: Tips and Tricks for Beginners is your ultimate guide to navigating the enchanting wonders of this iconic destination. In this book, we will unlock the secrets and unveil the hidden gems that make Disneyland Paris truly magical.

From the moment you step foot in this captivating wonderland, we will be your steadfast companion, guiding you through the intricacies of this mesmerising realm.

But before we delve into the depths of Disneyland Paris, let us take a moment to marvel at the rich tapestry of history that surrounds this extraordinary place.

Did you know that Disneyland Paris first opened its gates in 1992, making it the second Disney park to be built outside of the United

States? Over the years, it has become a beloved destination for millions of visitors from all corners of the globe, drawing them in with its captivating blend of fairy tales and thrills.

As you embark on your journey through the pages of this book, be prepared to unlock the secrets of Disneyland Paris like never before. We will navigate the winding streets of Main Street, U.S.A., where the nostalgia of yesteryear melds with the promise of a brighter future.
We will witness the mesmerising parades that bring beloved characters to life, their vibrant costumes and infectious energy igniting the hearts of all who witness their procession.

But Disneyland Paris is more than just a park; it is an entire universe waiting to be explored. We will venture beyond the confines of the magical kingdom and discover the hidden gems that lie within the surrounding area.
From charming local hotels that offer a respite from the hustle and bustle of the park to delectable culinary delights that tantalise the taste buds, we will unveil the best-kept secrets that make Disneyland Paris a true haven for both the young and the young at heart.

Join me, as we embark on a journey of discovery and wonder. Together, we will navigate the intricate tapestry of Disneyland Paris, unearthing its treasures and unveiling its mysteries. Whether you seek the thrill of roller coasters or the tranquility of a leisurely stroll through beautifully manicured gardens, Disneyland Paris offers something for everyone.

So pack your bags, fasten your seatbelts, and prepare to embark on an adventure that will ignite your imagination and create memories that will last a lifetime.

Let Discovering Disneyland Paris: Tips and Tricks for Beginners be your compass as you navigate the wonders of this extraordinary destination. The magic awaits, and it is time to begin.

CHAPTER 1

A Magical Destination Unveiled

As you step through the grand entrance of Disneyland Paris, you're transported to a world where dreams come true and childhood fantasies are brought to life. But before we delve into the enchanting wonders that await you, let's take a moment to uncover the fascinating history of this iconic destination.

It all began in the early 1980s when the Walt Disney Company set its sights on expanding the magic of Disneyland to Europe. After carefully considering various locations, the picturesque countryside of Marne-la-Vallee, just outside Paris, was chosen as the perfect setting for the park. And thus, Disneyland Paris was born.

Opening its gates on April 12, 1992, Disneyland Paris immediately captured the hearts of visitors from near and far. This magical destination quickly became a symbol of joy, imagination, and wonder, captivating the minds of both young and old. Its success not only established it as one of the top tourist attractions in Europe but also paved the way for future Disney parks around the world.But what sets Disneyland Paris apart from its counterparts?

It's the perfect blend of Disney's signature storytelling and European charm. From the moment you enter the park, you'll notice a seamless integration of Disney's classic tales and the rich history and culture of France. It's like a marriage of fairy tales and French savoir-faire, creating a truly unique experience.

As you stroll down Main Street, U.S.A., with its quaint Victorian architecture and charming boutiques, you'll be transported back in time to an era of horse-drawn carriages and gas lamps. And as you venture further into the park, you'll find yourself immersed in the enchanting worlds of beloved Disney films.

From the breathtaking castle of Sleeping Beauty to the swashbuckling adventures of Pirates of the Caribbean, each land offers its own brand of magic.But Disneyland Paris is not just about the attractions. It's a place where dreams come true for all your senses. The aroma of freshly baked pastries wafts through the air, beckoning you to indulge in delectable treats from around the world. From the rich flavours of French cuisine to the whimsical delights of Mickey-shaped ice creams, there's something to satisfy every craving.

And let's not forget the parades and night-time shows that illuminate the park with dazzling lights and breathtaking performances. Whether it's the magical parade of Disney characters dancing through the streets or the spectacular fireworks extravaganza illuminating the night sky, these captivating spectacles will leave you awe-inspired and filled with joy.

Now, as you embark on your adventure in Disneyland Paris, remember to keep your eyes peeled for hidden gems. From secret paths that lead to unexpected discoveries to lesser-known attractions that often have shorter queues, these hidden treasures can add an extra sprinkle of magic to your visit.

So, grab your mouse ears, put on your most comfortable walking shoes, and get ready to be whisked away into a world of enchantment. Disneyland Paris awaits, ready to make your dreams come true.

And remember, as Walt Disney himself once said, "Laughter is timeless, imagination has no age, and dreams are forever."

Enough of the history lesson, let's dive into the practicalities of making the most out of your Disneyland Paris adventure.

And trust me, at Disneyland Paris, you'll be over the moon with all the magic and laughter that awaits you.

So, buckle up and get ready for the ride of a lifetime!

Getting Started

Welcome to the magical world of Disneyland Paris! Whether you're a wide-eyed child or a child-at-heart, this guide is here to ensure that your first trip to the park is a memorable one. We'll cover everything you need to know to make the most of your experience, from planning your trip to navigating the park like a seasoned pro.

First things first, let's talk about planning.

Disneyland Paris offers a multitude of attractions and entertainment options, so it's essential to do your research before you go. Start by checking the park's official website, where you'll find up-to-date information on park hours, special events, and even some handy tips and tricks. Trust me, you'll thank yourself later for taking the time to plan ahead.

Now, let's delve into the nitty-gritty details. When it comes to accommodations, Disneyland Paris has a wide range of options to suit every budget.

From luxurious onsite hotels to cosy offsite accommodations, there's something for everyone. If you want to be right in the heart of the magic, I highly recommend staying at one of the Disneyland Paris hotels. Not only will you be just steps away from the park, but you'll also enjoy exclusive perks like early access to the park and character meet-and-greets.Speaking of characters, let's not forget about the hidden gems at the park. While everyone knows about Mickey and Minnie, there are plenty of lesser-known characters just waiting to make your acquaintance.

Keep an eye out for the elusive Figment or the mischievous Cheshire Cat. Trust me, meeting these characters will add an extra sprinkle of magic to your trip.Now, let's talk about sustenance.

Disneyland Paris is not just a feast for the eyes but also for the taste buds. From delectable Mickey-shaped treats to mouthwatering French pastries, the park offers a culinary adventure like no other. Don't miss the chance to indulge in a croissant at Café Fantasia or enjoy a romantic dinner at the Ratatouille-themed restaurant. Just remember to pace yourself - there's plenty of deliciousness to go around!
Of course, no trip to Disneyland Paris would be complete without experiencing the iconic parades and night-time shows. Picture this: dazzling floats, colourful costumes, and your favourite Disney characters dancing to catchy tunes. It's a spectacle that will leave you in awe and make you want to sing along at the top of your lungs. Oh, and did I mention the fireworks? Prepare to be dazzled as the night sky lights up with a symphony of colours and sparkles.Now that you're practically bursting with excitement, let's talk about how to get to Disneyland Paris.

The park is conveniently located just a short distance from the heart of Paris, making it easily accessible by train, bus, or even car. If you're feeling adventurous, why not take a scenic boat ride along the Seine River? It's a unique way to kick off your Disney adventure.

Before I wrap up this segment, let me leave you with a joke to keep the smiles going. Why did Mickey Mouse go to outer space? Because he wanted to find Pluto! I know, I know, it's cheesy, but it's guaranteed to bring a smile to your face, just like your upcoming trip to Disneyland Paris.So there you have it, a taste of what's to come in your Disneyland Paris adventure. Whether you're a seasoned traveler or a first-time visitor, this guide will be your trusty companion throughout your journey.

So fasten your seatbelts, put on your Mickey ears, and get ready to embark on the trip of a lifetime. The magic awaits!

Navigating the Parks

As you step foot into the magical realm of Disneyland Paris, you may feel a surge of excitement and wonder. But amidst all the dazzling attractions and characters, you might find yourself lost in a sea of people, searching for your next adventure. Fear not, my fellow traveller, for I shall be your trusty guide through the labyrinthine layout of Disneyland Paris!

First things first, let's tackle the geography of the park. Disneyland Paris is divided into two main sections: Disneyland Park and Walt Disney Studios Park. The former is the classic Disneyland experience, with iconic attractions like Sleeping Beauty's Castle and the thrilling Space Mountain. The latter is a more behind-the-scenes look at the magic of Disney, with attractions inspired by beloved movies like Ratatouille and Toy Story.

Within each park, you'll find different lands or areas that transport you to different worlds. From the enchanting Main Street, U.S.A. to the wild jungles of Adventureland, each land has its unique charm and attractions. Take note of these lands, my dear reader, as they will be your navigational compass throughout your adventure.Now, let's talk about some tips and tricks for finding your way around.

One of the best tools at your disposal is the park map. It's like a treasure map, guiding you to your heart's desires. Grab one at the entrance or download the Disneyland Paris app, which not only provides maps but also real-time wait times for attractions. Trust me, knowing the wait times for that coveted ride can save you from endless queues and keep your mood as sunny as a day in Fantasyland.Speaking of queues, be prepared for them.

Disneyland Paris is a popular destination, and you'll often find yourself in line for your favourite attractions. But fear not! This is the perfect opportunity to strike up a conversation with your fellow Disney enthusiasts. Who knows, you might just make some lifelong friends while waiting for Pirates of the Caribbean!

As you wander through the park, keep an eye out for signs and landmarks.

Disneyland Paris has a fantastic system of signage that will guide you to your desired destination. And if you ever find yourself disoriented, simply look up and find the majestic Sleeping Beauty Castle. It's like a North Star, guiding lost souls back on track.Now, let's talk about one of my favourite subjects – food! Disneyland Paris offers a wide variety of dining options, from quick bites to fancy feasts. But navigating the world of dining can be overwhelming, especially when your stomach is growling louder than a parade of marching band. My advice? Try a bit of everything!

Indulge in a croissant at a charming café on Main Street, U.S.A., savour a gooey caramel apple in Fantasyland, and have a romantic dinner in the heart of Ratatouille's Paris. Remember, calories don't count in the land of Disney!

Lastly, don't forget to immerse yourself in the magical parades and night-time shows that Disneyland Paris has to offer. These spectacular displays of lights, music, and beloved characters will leave you in awe and remind you why you embarked on this Disney adventure in the first place. So grab a spot early, make some friends, and let the enchantment wash over you.

And there you have it, my dear reader – a guide to navigating the parks of Disneyland Paris. With a map in hand, a sense of adventure in your heart, and a sprinkle of Disney magic, you are ready to conquer this magical kingdom. So go forth, explore, and remember to always keep your eyes open for hidden Mickey's and hidden gems. After all, the true magic of Disneyland Paris lies in the unexpected surprises that await around every corner.

Choosing the Best Time to Visit

When it comes to planning your magical trip to Disneyland Paris, one of the most crucial decisions you'll make is choosing the best time to visit. Trust me, you don't want to be caught in a sea of Minnie Mouse ears during peak season or miss out on the enchanting Christmas festivities by visiting in the scorching heat of summer. So, let's dive right into the seasons and events at Disneyland Paris to help you plan your trip accordingly.

Spring:As the flowers bloom and the sun shines a little brighter, springtime at Disneyland Paris is a truly enchanting experience. From late March to early June, you can bask in the beauty of the park as it comes alive with vibrant colours and joyful energy. Plus, the weather is just perfect – not too hot, not too cold.
It's like Goldilocks found the perfect season!But wait, there's more! Springtime also brings special events to the park.
The Festival of Pirates and Princesses is a swashbuckling adventure where you can choose your side and join in the festivities. Are you more of a Jack Sparrow or a Cinderella kind of person? The choice is yours, matey!

Summer:Ah, summer. The time for ice cream, sunburns, and endless queues. If you're a fan of long lines and sweaty crowds, then visiting Disneyland Paris during the summer months is just for you. But hey, let's not be too negative.
Summer does have its perks!Firstly, the weather is warm and sunny, perfect for enjoying the outdoor attractions and catching some rays. Secondly, summer is the time for the famous Disney Nighttime Spectaculars. Picture this: a starry sky, Cinderella Castle aglow, and a breathtaking fireworks display.

Autumn:As the leaves change colours and a crisp breeze fills the air, autumn at Disneyland Paris is a sight to behold. From September to November, the park transforms into a fall wonderland, complete with pumpkins, scarecrows, and all things Halloween. Boo to you!During this time, you can experience the spine-tingling thrills of the Halloween Festival. From spooky parades to haunted attractions,
Disneyland Paris takes Halloween to a whole new level. And don't worry, they have a range of costumes for both the brave and the scaredy-cats out there. Who said Disneyland Paris was just for kids?

Winter:Winter at Disneyland Paris is truly magical. From November to February, the park gets a sprinkle of pixie dust and transforms into a winter wonderland. Think snow-covered castles, twinkling lights, and the jingle of Christmas carols filling the air.If you're a fan of the holiday season, then visiting Disneyland Paris during winter is an absolute must. The park goes all out with their Christmas celebrations, from stunning decorations to festive parades and shows.
And let's not forget about meeting the big guy himself – Santa Claus! Whether you're on the naughty or nice list, he's always up for a selfie.Now that you have a glimpse of the seasons and events at Disneyland Paris, it's time to plan your trip accordingly.

Remember, each season has its own unique charm and offerings. Whether you're a fan of springtime blooms, summer spectacles, autumnal chills, or winter wonderlands, Disneyland Paris has something for everyone.

So, grab your Mickey ears, pack your sense of adventure, and get ready for a trip of a lifetime.

And remember, no matter what time of year you choose to visit, the magic of Disneyland Paris will always be there to welcome you with open arms (and Mickey-shaped waffles).

Park Tickets and Passes

Please note as of late July 2023 DISNEYLAND Paris is introducing a new system for annual pass holders and new pricing. Please check this directly on the site for up to date information.

As you step foot into the magical world of Disneyland Paris, one of the first things you'll need to consider is how to make the most of your visit by choosing the right park tickets and passes. With a multitude of options available, it's essential to have a clear understanding of what each ticket offers and how it can enhance your experience.Let's start with the basics - the park tickets.

Disneyland Paris offers a range of ticket options, from single-day tickets to multi-day tickets. The single-day ticket grants you access to one of the two parks - Disneyland Park or Walt Disney Studios Park - for a full day of adventure and excitement. If you're planning to immerse yourself in the magic for multiple days, the multi-day tickets are your best bet. These tickets allow you to hop between both parks, giving you the freedom to explore everything Disneyland Paris has to offer.

Now, let's dive into the world of annual passes. If you're a true Disney enthusiast or planning to visit Disneyland Paris multiple times in a year, an annual pass is a fantastic option. With different tiers to choose from, each pass offers a variety of perks and benefits. From unlimited park entry to exclusive discounts on merchandise and dining, an annual pass is your golden ticket to endless Disney magic. Just imagine being able to experience the thrill of Space Mountain or the enchantment of Sleeping Beauty Castle whenever you please!But wait, there's more! Disneyland Paris also offers special passes for certain events and seasons.

From Halloween-themed parties to dazzling Christmas celebrations, these passes grant you access to unique experiences that will leave you in awe. Whether you're craving the chills of Phantom Manor during Halloween or dreaming of a white

Christmas with the magical Disney Parade, these special passes are your gateway to unforgettable memories.

Now, let's talk about how to make the most of your visit with these tickets and passes. Planning is key!

Take the time to research the park's schedule, including parade and show timings, so you can optimise your day and catch all the must-see attractions. And don't forget to take advantage of the Premier Access system, which allows you to skip the queues for popular rides and make the most of your time in the park.

Another tip to maximise your visit is to explore the hidden gems of Disneyland Paris. While iconic attractions like It's a Small World and Pirates of the Caribbean are a must, there are also lesser-known gems waiting to be discovered.

From the whimsical Alice's Curious Labyrinth to the thrilling Ratatouille: The Adventure, these hidden gems offer unique experiences that will leave you enchanted.When it comes to food and drink, Disneyland Paris has a feast for your taste buds. From delicious Mickey-shaped waffles to mouthwatering French pastries, there's something to satisfy every craving. And don't forget to try the iconic Dole Whip - a refreshing pineapple-flavoured soft serve that is an absolute must-try!

Lastly, let's talk about getting there. Disneyland Paris is easily accessible by various modes of transportation. Whether you choose to travel by train, bus, or car, the park is well-connected and conveniently located. And if you're staying at one of the onsite or surrounding area hotels, you can take advantage of the park's shuttle service for a hassle-free journey.

Remember, choosing the right ticket option or annual pass can truly enhance your visit and make it a truly unforgettable experience.

So go ahead, grab your tickets, and get ready to embark on a magical adventure filled with laughter, joy, and plenty of Disney magic!

CHAPTER 2

Accommodation

Disneyland Paris Hotels

Overview of the official Disney hotels and their unique themes and benefitsWhen it comes to planning a trip to Disneyland Paris, finding the perfect place to rest your weary feet after a day of magical adventures is key.

Luckily, Disneyland Paris offers a range of official Disney hotels that not only provide a comfortable stay but also transport you into a world of enchantment. Let's take a closer look at these hotels and their unique themes and benefits.

1. Disneyland Hotel: As the grand dame of Disney hotels, the Disneyland Hotel is a sight to behold. With its stunning Victorian architecture and luxurious interiors, it exudes elegance and charm. Imagine stepping into a fairytale as you enter the lobby adorned with sparkling chandeliers and intricate details. And don't forget to keep an eye out for Mickey Mouse, who often makes appearances to greet guests. Plus, staying at the Disneyland Hotel grants you the exclusive privilege of early access to the Disneyland Park, allowing you to beat the crowds and make the most of your magical day. ***Reopening in 2024***

2. Disney's Hotel New York - The Art of Marvel: If you're a Marvel fan, then this hotel is an absolute must-stay. Recently transformed into a haven for superheroes, the hotel celebrates

the world of Marvel with its contemporary and stylish design. From the moment you step into the lobby, you'll be immersed in the dynamic art of Marvel, with larger-than-life statues and vibrant murals. And let's not forget about the Iron Man-themed Stark's Bar, where you can enjoy a cocktail and unleash your inner superhero. This hotel is a true paradise for Marvel enthusiasts.

3. Disney's Newport Bay Club: For those seeking a nautical escape, Disney's Newport Bay Club is the perfect choice. Inspired by the charm of New England seaside resorts, this hotel offers a tranquil retreat after a day of excitement in the parks. The rooms are elegantly decorated with a touch of maritime flair, and the panoramic views of Lake Disney are simply breathtaking. One of the unique benefits of staying at Disney's Newport Bay Club is the opportunity to take a relaxing boat ride to the parks, allowing you to start your day with a touch of serenity.

4. Disney's Sequoia Lodge: If you yearn for the beauty of nature, Disney's Sequoia Lodge is the ideal hotel for you. Nestled amidst towering sequoia trees, this rustic lodge exudes a cozy and welcoming atmosphere. The lobby, with its roaring fireplace and comfortable seating areas, invites you to unwind and enjoy the tranquility. The rooms are adorned with warm, earthy tones, providing a peaceful haven to recharge. And don't forget to explore the hotel grounds, where you'll discover beautiful gardens and even a hidden waterfall. It's the perfect retreat for nature lovers.

5. Disney's Hotel Cheyenne: For those with a love for the Wild West, Disney's Hotel Cheyenne will transport you straight into the heart of cowboy country. This hotel captures the essence of the Old West, with its rustic buildings and Western-themed decor. From the moment you step into the saloon-style reception area, you'll feel like a cowboy or cowgirl ready to embark on an adventure. The rooms feature playful cowboy motifs, and you'll even find a Sheriff Woody statue in the courtyard. It's the perfect hotel for little cowpokes and adults alike.

No matter which Disney hotel you choose, you'll be treated to the renowned Disney service and attention to detail. Each hotel offers a range of amenities, including themed restaurants, pools, and easy access to the parks. Plus, staying at an official Disney hotel comes with some extra perks, such as Extra Magic Time, where you can enter the parks before they open to the general public.

So, whether you're dreaming of a fairytale castle, an encounter with your favourite superheroes, a serene lakeside retreat, a cozy lodge in the woods, or an adventure in the Wild West, Disneyland Paris has a hotel to suit every taste and preference.

So, grab your Mickey ears, pack your bags, and get ready for a truly magical stay. As Walt Disney once said, "If you can dream it, you can do it" – and at Disneyland Paris hotels, dreams really do come true.

And remember, if you hear a duck quacking in the hallway, don't worry, it's just Donald Duck trying to find his room!

Offsite Accommodation

When it comes to planning your trip to Disneyland Paris, one of the most important decisions you'll make is where to stay. While the onsite hotels offer convenience and that magical Disney experience, sometimes it's nice to venture offsite and explore what the surrounding area has to offer.

Luckily, there are plenty of options for all budgets when it comes to offsite accommodation near Disneyland Paris.For the budget-conscious traveler, there are a variety of affordable hotels located just a stone's throw away from the park. One such option is the delightful "Mickey's Budget Inn," where you'll feel like a true Disney insider without breaking the bank. The rooms may not be the largest, but they are cozy and clean, and the staff is always eager to sprinkle a little extra pixie dust on your stay.

Plus, you'll be just a short walk or a quick shuttle ride away from the park entrance.If you're looking for something a bit more upscale, consider the "Dream Castle Hotel." This luxurious resort is fit for royalty, with its regal architecture and opulent rooms. The onsite restaurant offers delectable cuisine fit for a king or queen, and the spa is the perfect place to unwind after a long day of exploring the park. You may even spot a Disney princess or two enjoying a well-deserved pampering session.

Just be sure to book early, as this enchanting getaway fills up quickly.For those who prefer a more home-away-from-home experience, there are a plethora of vacation rentals available near Disneyland Paris. Whether you're traveling with a large family or just want the extra space to spread out, these rentals provide all the comforts of home with a touch of Disney magic. Imagine waking up in a cozy cottage just minutes away from the park, enjoying breakfast on your private terrace, and then heading out for a day of Disney adventures. It's like having your own little slice of the Magic Kingdom.

Remember, when choosing your offsite accommodation near Disneyland Paris, consider your budget, preferences, and the type of experience you're looking for. Whether you opt for a budget-friendly hotel, a luxurious resort, or a cozy vacation rental, you're sure to find the perfect home base for your magical Disney adventure.

Happy travels, and may your offsite stay be filled with pixie dust and unforgettable memories!

Transportation to the Parks

When it comes to getting to Disneyland Paris, you have more options than you can shake a Mickey Mouse-shaped stick at. So, let's hop aboard the Disney Express and explore the various transportation options available to reach the park and travel within it. Buckle up, folks, because this is going to be a wild ride! First things first, let's talk about getting to Disneyland Paris.

If you're arriving by plane, you'll most likely be landing at either Charles de Gaulle Airport or Orly Airport. Don't worry, Disney has got you covered with their magical transportation services. You can hop on the Magical Shuttle, which will whisk you away to the park in no time. And let me tell you, there's nothing quite like starting your Disney adventure with a shuttle that's straight out of a fairytale.Now, if you're a fan of trains (choo-choo!), then you're in luck.

Disneyland Paris has its very own train station conveniently located right at the park. Talk about a grand entrance! The high-speed TGV train can take you directly to Marne-la-Vallée/Chessy station, which is just a hop, skip, and a jump away from the magic. Plus, you'll feel like a real-life Disney character as you glide into the station amidst a cloud of pixie dust (okay, maybe not actual pixie dust, but a sprinkle of imagination goes a long way).But wait, there's more! If you're feeling fancy (and who doesn't want to feel fancy when going to Disneyland?), you can opt for a private transfer. Picture this: a luxurious car, a chauffeur in a dapper suit, and the wind in your hair as you make your grand entrance at the park. It's like stepping into your very own fairytale, where the only pumpkin you'll see is the one turned into a magical carriage.

Now, I know what you're thinking. "What about walking? Can I just stroll from one land to another?"
Well, my dear Disney enthusiast, you absolutely can! Disneyland Paris is designed to be easily walkable, with each land seamlessly connected to the next. So, lace up your walking shoes and embark on a magical adventure as you explore the park at your own pace.And there you have it, folks. A whirlwind tour of the transportation options available to reach Disneyland Paris and travel within the park.

Whether you choose to arrive in style in a private transfer, glide in on the Disney Express, or take a leisurely train ride around the park, one thing is for sure – your journey to the happiest place on earth will be nothing short of magical.

Choosing the Right Hotel:

When it comes to planning a trip, one of the most crucial decisions you'll make is choosing the right hotel. A good hotel can make your vacation a dream come true, while a bad one can turn it into a nightmare. So, buckle up and let's dive into the factors you should consider when selecting a hotel based on location, amenities, and convenience.First and foremost, let's talk about location. Picture this: you've just spent the whole day exploring the magical wonders of Disneyland Paris, and your feet are begging for mercy. The last thing you want is a long, tiring journey back to your hotel. So, when choosing a hotel, make sure it's conveniently located near the park.

This way, you can easily hop on a shuttle or take a short walk back to your cozy haven, where a fluffy bed awaits your tired body.But location isn't just about proximity to the park. It's also about what's around the hotel. You'll want to consider factors like nearby restaurants, shopping centres, and other attractions. After all, Disneyland Paris isn't the only place worth exploring. So, choose a hotel that gives you easy access to the best of both worlds - the enchantment of the park and the vibrant life outside its gates.Now, let's talk about amenities. When you're on vacation, you deserve to be treated like royalty. So, look for hotels that offer a wide range of amenities to make your stay truly magical. Whether it's a swimming pool to cool off after a long day of adventures or a spa to relax those tired muscles, these little luxuries can make all the difference. And let's not forget the importance of a hearty breakfast buffet to fuel up for a day of excitement. Trust me, Mickey-shaped waffles taste even better when they're included in your hotel package.

Lastly, let's not overlook convenience. When you're exploring the magical world of Disneyland Paris, the last thing you want is to waste precious time on mundane tasks. So, choose a hotel that offers convenient services like ticket purchasing, transportation arrangements, and even character meet-and-greets right in the lobby. Imagine starting your day with a cup of coffee and a warm hug from Mickey Mouse himself. Talk about starting the day off on the right foot!Now, let's sprinkle in some jokes to keep things light-hearted.

Choosing the right hotel is like finding your Prince Charming in a sea of frogs. You want a hotel that makes you feel like a princess, not one that leaves you feeling like a pumpkin carriage at midnight. So, remember to do your research, read reviews, and choose wisely. After all, your hotel should be your home away from home, where dreams come true and sleep is as magical as a happily ever after.In conclusion, when choosing the right hotel for your Disneyland Paris adventure, consider factors like location, amenities, and convenience. You deserve a hotel that is not only close to the park but also offers a range of luxurious amenities to make your stay unforgettable. And don't forget, convenience is key - choose a hotel that takes care of the little things, so you can focus on making lifelong memories.

So, go forth, my fellow travellers, and find that perfect hotel that will be your own personal gateway to the enchantment of Disneyland Paris. Happy hunting, and may the magic be with you!

Deals and Packages
When it comes to planning a trip to Disneyland Paris, finding the best deals, discounts, and package options for accommodations is like discovering hidden treasures in the park itself. It requires a

keen eye, a touch of luck, and a sprinkle of magic. But fear not, my fellow adventurers, for I am here to guide you through this mystical realm of money-saving possibilities!First and foremost, let's talk about the Disneyland Paris website. This is your portal to the enchanted kingdom, where dreams come true and discounts are waiting to be found. The website often offers exclusive deals and packages that can save you a princely sum.

So, make sure to check it regularly and keep your eyes peeled for those golden opportunities.Now, let me share with you a little secret. Sometimes, the best deals are not found within the confines of the kingdom itself, but in the surrounding lands. Yes, my friends, I'm talking about off-site accommodations. These hidden gems can offer lower rates and extra perks that will make your journey even more enchanting. Don't be afraid to venture outside the park and explore the neighbouring towns for charming hotels and cozy bed and breakfasts. Trust me, it's worth the extra effort!

But if you prefer to stay within the embrace of the kingdom, fear not, for there are still deals to be found. One option is to book your accommodations directly through the Disneyland Paris website. They often have special offers and package deals that include not only your stay but also park tickets, dining vouchers, and even magical extras like character meet-and-greets. It's like a treasure chest filled with discounts and surprises!

Now, let's talk about timing. Timing is everything, my dear adventurers. If you can be flexible with your travel dates, you may stumble upon some truly magical deals. Off-peak seasons, weekdays, and even certain months can offer lower rates and fewer crowds. It's like having the park all to yourself, but with a smaller dent in your purse.But wait, there's more! If you're a savvy traveler who loves a good bargain, consider becoming a Disneyland Paris annual pass holder (Changing July 2023, please check the official website). With this magical pass in hand, you'll not only have unlimited access to the park but also enjoy exclusive discounts on accommodations, dining, and merchandise. It's like having a golden ticket to a world of savings!

Now, let's sprinkle some humour into this magical adventure, shall we?

Finding the best deals, discounts, and package options for accommodations at Disneyland Paris is a quest worth embarking on. Whether you choose to explore off-site options, dive into the treasure trove of deals on the Disneyland Paris website, or become an annual pass holder, there are savings to be had and memories to be made.

And remember, as you embark on this journey, always keep a little extra pixie dust in your pocket. You never know when it might come in handy!

CHAPTER 3

Exploring the Parks

Main Street, U.S.A.

Main Street at Disneyland Paris is an iconic and charming entry point to the magical world of the park. Designed to evoke the nostalgic ambiance of early 20th-century small-town America, Main Street immerses visitors in a bygone era with its meticulously crafted architecture, delightful shops, and lively atmosphere. Let's delve into Main Street at Disneyland Paris.

Setting and Design:
Main Street is the first area visitors encounter upon entering Disneyland Paris. It serves as the main thoroughfare leading towards Sleeping Beauty Castle, the centrepiece of the park. The design draws inspiration from the Victorian and Edwardian architectural styles prevalent in the United States during the early 20th century. The facades of the buildings lining Main Street showcase intricate details, colourful facades, and charming storefronts, inviting guests into a world of wonder and exploration.

Welcoming Atmosphere:
Main Street exudes a warm and welcoming atmosphere, transporting guests to a simpler time. The street is bustling with activity, with the sound of cheerful ragtime tunes playing in the background. Horse-drawn carriages and vintage vehicles traverse the street, adding to the nostalgic charm. The scent of freshly baked pastries from the Main

Street Bakery fills the air, enticing visitors to indulge in delightful treats.

Shops and Dining:
Main Street is home to an array of unique shops, offering a variety of merchandise to suit every taste. Emporium, the largest store on Main Street, features an extensive selection of Disney-themed merchandise, including apparel, accessories, collectibles, and souvenirs. Other shops include Harrington's Fine China & Porcelains, where guests can find elegant tableware, and Main Street Motors, offering die-cast model cars and vintage-inspired decor.

For dining, Main Street offers a range of options to satisfy every craving. Casey's Corner, a classic American-style eatery, serves up hot dogs and other delicious ballpark favourites. Plaza Gardens Restaurant provides a buffet-style dining experience with an international menu. The Gibson Girl Ice Cream Parlor entices guests with a mouthwatering selection of ice cream flavours, perfect for a sweet indulgence.

Entertainment and Attractions:
Main Street provides captivating entertainment that adds to the overall charm. The Main Street Philharmonic, a talented brass and percussion ensemble, performs lively tunes throughout the day, filling the street with joyous melodies. The Dapper Dans, a barbershop quartet, captivate audiences with their harmonious singing and witty banter.

While Main Street itself does not host major attractions, it serves as a gateway to the enchanting wonders of Disneyland Paris. Visitors can take a leisurely stroll down Main Street, soaking in the ambiance, before embarking on their adventures in the various themed lands that lie beyond.

Parades and Events:
Main Street comes alive during parades and special events. The daily parade, such as Disney Stars on Parade, showcases beloved Disney characters on vibrant floats, accompanied by energetic music

and dance routines. Additionally, during seasonal celebrations like Halloween and Christmas, Main Street transforms with festive decorations, illuminations, and themed entertainment, creating a truly enchanting experience for guests of all ages.

Hidden Gems:
Main Street is brimming with hidden gems and delightful details. Keep an eye out for the Main Street Windows, dedicated to the individuals who have made significant contributions to the development and success of Disneyland Paris. These windows feature whimsical names and occupations, offering a nod to the rich history of the park.

Main Street at Disneyland Paris captures the essence of small-town America from a bygone era. With its meticulously designed architecture, charming shops, delightful dining options, and lively atmosphere, Main Street sets the stage for the magical adventures that await visitors in the rest of the park. It is a place where nostalgia and imagination intertwine, creating cherished memories for guests of all ages.

City Hall

First-time visitors to Disneyland Paris can seek assistance and support from City Hall, also known as Guest Relations. City Hall is located near the entrance of Disneyland Park and provides a range of services to ensure a smooth and enjoyable experience.

Here are some of the services and assistance that guests can expect from City Hall:

1. Information and Guidance: City Hall is staffed with knowledgeable cast members who can provide detailed information about the park, attractions, entertainment schedules, dining options, and more. They can offer guidance on navigating the park and answer any questions you may have.

2. Lost and Found: If you misplace or lose an item during your visit,

you can report it at City Hall. They maintain a lost and found service to help reunite guests with their belongings whenever possible.

3. Guest Assistance and Accessibility: City Hall offers support and services for guests with disabilities or special needs. They can provide information on accessible attractions, facilities, and services, as well as assist with any specific requirements or accommodations.

4. Premier Pass Assistance: Premier Pass is a system that allows guests to reserve a specific time slot to experience popular attractions with reduced wait times. City Hall can provide guidance on how to obtain and use Premier Pass effectively, maximising your time in the park.

5. Celebration Buttons: City Hall is the place to go to celebrate special occasions. They offer complimentary celebration buttons for birthdays, anniversaries, and other milestones. Wearing these buttons can add a touch of extra magic to your visit, as cast members and other guests may extend warm wishes and greetings.

6. General Assistance and Concerns: Should you have any general concerns, feedback, or specific needs during your visit, City Hall is there to assist. They will do their best to address any issues and ensure that your Disneyland Paris experience is as enjoyable as possible.

Remember to approach City Hall with any questions, concerns, or requests for assistance during your visit.

The friendly and helpful cast members are dedicated to ensuring your time at Disneyland Paris is memorable and filled with magic.

Adventureland

Adventureland at Disneyland Paris is a captivating and immersive land that invites visitors to embark on thrilling expeditions and discover the wonders of distant lands. Let's explore Adventureland in this write-up, including information on its rides, hidden features, and more.

Theme and Setting:
Adventureland transports guests to exotic locales, evoking the spirit of exploration and adventure. The land is designed to resemble a lush tropical jungle, complete with dense foliage, ancient ruins, and mysterious pathways. From the moment visitors step foot into Adventureland, they are enveloped in a sense of intrigue and anticipation.

Attractions and Rides:
Adventureland offers a range of exciting attractions and rides that cater to adventurers of all ages. Here are some notable experiences:

Pirates of the Caribbean: Embark on a swashbuckling journey through a Caribbean pirate haven. This classic boat ride takes guests through dark caves, eerie grottos, and pirate-infested waters, immersing them in a world of pirates, treasure, and adventure.

Indiana Jones™ and the Temple of Peril: Join Indiana Jones on a daring roller coaster expedition. This thrilling ride takes passengers through a temple ruin, filled with twists, turns, and unexpected surprises. Brace yourself for an exhilarating adventure!

Adventure Isle: Explore Adventure Isle, a lush and sprawling area filled with hidden caves, suspension bridges, and cascading waterfalls. Guests can navigate the Swiss Family Robinson Treehouse, cross the perilous rope bridge to the Skull Rock, and discover secret passages amidst the dense foliage.

Hidden Features and Details:
Adventureland is rich with hidden features and intricate details that enhance the immersive experience. Keep an eye out for these hidden gems:

Explorers Club: Near the entrance of Adventureland, you'll find the Colonel Hathi's Pizza Outpost. Look for the adjacent building, which houses the Explorers Club. Inside, you'll discover artefacts, maps, and curious items collected from around the world, providing a glimpse into the adventurous spirit of explorers.

Aladdin's Enchanted Passage: Delve into the world of Aladdin and explore the enchanting Enchanted Passage. This walk-through attraction showcases scenes from the beloved animated film, allowing guests to relive the magic and meet their favourite characters.

Adventureland Bazaar: Wander through the bustling marketplace of Adventureland Bazaar, where vibrant stalls and shops offer a variety of exotic merchandise. From unique souvenirs to traditional crafts, the Bazaar provides a feast for the senses.

Dining and Refreshments:
Adventureland offers diverse dining options to satisfy the cravings of intrepid explorers. Here are a few highlights:
Colonel Hathi's Pizza Outpost: Enjoy a break from your adventures with a selection of pizza, pasta, and refreshing drinks. The restaurant's vibrant setting, inspired by the Jungle Book, provides a delightful dining experience.

Hakuna Matata Restaurant: Step into this African-themed quick-service eatery and savour flavoursome dishes such as rotisserie chicken, vegetable couscous, and refreshing fruit salads. It's an ideal spot for a quick and satisfying meal.

Entertainment and Atmosphere:
Adventureland provides immersive entertainment that enhances the atmosphere and transports guests to far-off lands. Look out for live performances, streetmosphere characters, and musical experiences that capture the spirit of adventure.

Adventureland at Disneyland Paris offers a thrilling and immersive experience for explorers and adventurers. From the captivating rides like Pirates of the Caribbean and Indiana Jones™ and the Temple of Peril to the hidden features and details that add depth to the land's theme, Adventureland is a world of excitement and discovery.

Whether navigating through secret passages on Adventure Isle or savouring the flavours of exotic cuisine, this land invites guests to embark on unforgettable journeys and create lasting memories.

Fantasyland

Fantasyland at Disneyland Paris is a magical realm where fairy tales come to life. Filled with enchanting attractions, whimsical architecture, and beloved Disney characters, Fantasyland offers a captivating experience for guests of all ages.

Nestled in the heart of Disneyland Paris, this whimsical land is a must-visit for anyone seeking an escape into a world of fantasy and imagination.

From the moment you pass through the ornate entrance, adorned with intricate details and colourful banners, you'll feel the allure of this enchanting land pulling you deeper into its embrace.

Theme and Setting:
Fantasyland is designed as a charming and enchanting fairytale village, transporting visitors into the magical worlds of classic Disney stories. The architecture draws inspiration from European fairy tales, featuring turreted castles, colourful cottages, and elaborate facades. As guests step into Fantasyland, they are immersed in a world of fantasy, where dreams become reality.

Attractions and Rides:
Fantasyland is home to a variety of attractions that bring beloved Disney stories to life. Here are some notable experiences:

Sleeping Beauty Castle:
One of the first sights that will capture your attention is Sleeping Beauty Castle, standing tall and majestic at the centre of Fantasyland. This iconic landmark serves as a beacon, guiding visitors through

the various realms of magic and wonder that await them. With its stunning architecture and intricate storytelling, the castle is not just a photo opportunity, but a gateway to a world of adventure.

Guests can explore the castle's enchanting interior, featuring stunning stained glass windows and a gallery depicting the story of Sleeping Beauty.

It's a Small World: Embark on a delightful boat ride that takes you through the enchanting world of singing dolls representing different cultures from around the globe. The attraction's iconic theme song and colourful scenes make it a beloved classic.

Peter Pan's Flight: Join Peter Pan on a magical journey over the rooftops of London and into Neverland. This beloved dark ride takes guests on a flying pirate ship adventure, complete with stunning scenes and special effects.

Dumbo the Flying Elephant: Soar high above Fantasyland on the back of Dumbo, the famous flying elephant. This gentle carousel ride allows guests to control the height of their flying elephants, making it a favourite for younger visitors.

Hidden Features and Details:
Fantasyland is filled with hidden features and intricate details that add to the immersive experience. Look out for these hidden gems:

La Chaumière des Sept Nains: Venture into the charming cottage of Snow White's Seven Dwarfs. This walk-through attraction showcases scenes from the classic Disney film, including intricately carved woodwork and beautifully themed rooms.

Alice's Curious Labyrinth: Get lost in a maze inspired by Lewis Carroll's "Alice's Adventures in Wonderland." This interactive attraction allows guests to wander through the Queen of Hearts' garden, encounter characters from the story, and ultimately find their way to the Queen's Castle.

Le Pays des Contes de Fées: Board a whimsical boat and sail through a miniature landscape that brings to life scenes from various Disney fairy tales. From Cinderella's castle to the village of Belle, this enchanting journey offers a unique perspective on classic stories.

Dining and Refreshments:
Fantasyland offers a range of dining options to satisfy hungry adventurers. Here are a few highlights:
Auberge de Cendrillon: Step into a fairytale setting at this table-service restaurant inspired by Cinderella. Guests can enjoy a royal feast while mingling with Disney Princesses.

Toad Hall Restaurant: Located near the "Mr. Toad's Wild Ride" attraction, this quick-service restaurant serves British-inspired cuisine, including fish and chips and savoury pies. The whimsical decor adds to the charm of the dining experience.

Pizzeria Bella Notte: This quick-service restaurant is inspired by the iconic scene from Disney's "Lady and the Tramp." Guests can dine on pizza, pasta, and other Italian specialties while enjoying the charming ambiance of the restaurant.

Au Chalet de la Marionnette: Nestled near the "Pinocchio's Fantastic Journey" attraction, this quick-service eatery offers a selection of sandwiches, snacks, and refreshments. It's a convenient spot for a quick bite while exploring Fantasyland.

March Hare Refreshments: Located near the "Alice's Curious Labyrinth" attraction, this food kiosk offers a variety of snacks, beverages, and ice cream treats. It's a great spot to grab a quick refreshment while enjoying the whimsical atmosphere.

Cheshire Cat Café: This colorful food kiosk, inspired by the mischievous Cheshire Cat from "Alice in Wonderland," offers a selection of sweet treats, including pastries, muffins, and hot or cold drinks. It's a perfect spot for a quick sugar fix.

Additionally, Fantasyland features other food and beverage carts offering a range of snacks, drinks, and ice cream throughout the land.

These carts provide convenient options to satisfy your cravings while on the go.

It's important to note that dining options may vary, and it's always a good idea to check the park's official website or consult a park map for the most up-to-date information on available restaurants and food kiosks in Fantasyland.

Entertainment and Atmosphere:
Fantasyland provides additional entertainment and atmosphere to enhance the magical experience. Keep an eye out for character meet and greets, live shows, and musical performances that bring Disney stories to life right before your eyes.

Fantasyland at Disneyland Paris is a realm of enchantment and wonder, immersing guests in beloved Disney tales and offering a plethora of attractions and experiences. From iconic rides like It's a Small World and Peter Pan's Flight to hidden features and details that add depth to the land's theming, Fantasyland is a place where dreams come true.

Whether exploring Sleeping Beauty Castle, sailing through miniature storybook scenes, or enjoying a meal fit for royalty, this land captivates the imagination and creates cherished memories that will last a lifetime.

As you make your way through Fantasyland, be sure to take in the stunning sights and sounds that surround you. The vibrant colours, whimsical architecture, and captivating music create an atmosphere that is truly mesmerising.

Of course, no trip to Fantasyland would be complete without encountering some beloved Disney characters. From Mickey Mouse to Cinderella, you never know who you might run into as you explore this magical land. Keep your eyes peeled for impromptu meet and greets, where you can snap a photo with your favourite characters and create memories that will last a lifetime.

But Fantasyland isn't just about rides and attractions. It's a place where fairy tales come alive, and you can become a part of the stories you grew up with.

Frontierland

Welcome to Frontierland, where the wild west comes alive and the frontier spirit is infectious! In this thrilling segment of Disneyland Paris, you'll be transported back in time to the days of cowboys, saloons, and untamed wilderness. So put on your cowboy boots, grab your trusty lasso, and saddle up for an adventure like no other!

As you step into Frontierland, the first thing that will catch your eye is the incredible attention to detail. The buildings are designed to resemble an old western town, with rustic facades and wooden storefronts. You'll feel like you've stepped right into a John Wayne movie, with tumbleweeds rolling by and the sound of spurs jingling in the distance.

One of the highlights of Frontierland is the thrilling rides that will leave you breathless and wanting more. Take a journey on Big Thunder Mountain, a runaway mine train that will have you twisting and turning through canyons and caverns at breakneck speeds. Hold on tight as you navigate sharp turns and sudden drops, feeling the wind in your hair and the adrenaline pumping through your veins. It's a ride that will have you screaming "Yeehaw!" from start to finish.If you're in the mood for a more laid-back experience, hop aboard the Mark Twain Riverboat for a leisurely cruise along the Rivers of the Far West. As you glide along the calm waters, take in the stunning scenery of the American frontier.

Keep an eye out for wildlife, like the majestic bald eagle soaring overhead or the mischievous raccoons playing along the riverbanks. It's a peaceful and scenic journey that will transport you to a simpler time.But the fun doesn't stop at the rides - Frontierland also offers a variety of shows that will entertain and delight. Head over to the Lucky Nugget Saloon for the Buffalo Bill's Wild West Show, a spectacular dinner show that combines thrilling stunts, live animals, and good ol' western humour.

Watch in awe as cowboys and Native American warriors showcase their incredible riding skills, all while enjoying a hearty meal fit for a cowboy. It's a show that will have you clapping your hands and stomping your feet in true wild west fashion.

Now, I know what you're thinking - all this excitement is bound to make you hungry. Luckily, Frontierland has a range of dining options that will satisfy even the biggest appetites.

Dining and Refreshments:
Frontierland offers a range of dining options to satisfy hungry pioneers. Here are a few highlights:
Silver Spur Steakhouse: This table-service restaurant serves up delicious steaks and grilled specialties in a Western-themed setting. Guests can enjoy a hearty meal while immersing themselves in the atmosphere of the Old West.

Lucky Nugget Saloon: Step into this Western-style restaurant and enjoy a hearty meal in a rustic setting. The Lucky Nugget Saloon offers a selection of Tex-Mex cuisine, including barbecue dishes, burgers, and salads. Keep an eye out for live entertainment, including musical performances and can-can dancers.

Fuente del Oro Restaurante: Located near Big Thunder Mountain, this quick-service restaurant offers Mexican-inspired cuisine, including tacos, burritos, and nachos. It's a great spot for a quick and flavourful meal. (Whilst writing this book, this restaurant has now closed and is being made into a Coco themed restaurant (named Casa Del Coco) and will be open Summer 2023.)

Frontierland features other food and beverage carts offering a range of snacks, drinks, and ice cream throughout the land. These carts provide convenient options to satisfy your cravings while on the go.

Trust me, your taste buds will thank you.

As you explore Frontierland, keep an eye out for hidden gems that add an extra touch of magic to your experience. Look for the Boot Hill Cemetery, where the tombstones tell tales of the wild west, or visit the Rustler Roundup Shootin' Gallery for some old-fashioned target practice.

And don't forget to take a moment to relax and soak in the atmosphere at the Rivers of the Far West, where you can watch the steamboat go by and listen to the gentle sound of the water.Frontierland truly captures the essence of the wild west and the frontier spirit.
It's a place where adventure awaits around every corner and where you can let your imagination run wild. So whether you're a seasoned cowboy or a first-time wrangler, Frontierland is a must-visit destination that will leave you with memories to last a lifetime.

So saddle up, partner, and get ready to experience the wild west like never before! Happy trails, pardner!

Discoveryland

Discoveryland, the futuristic world of Disneyland Paris where technological wonders await! Step into a realm where imagination and innovation collide, and prepare to be awestruck by the marvels that lie before you.

As you enter Discoveryland, you'll immediately be transported to a time where the future meets the past. This unique blend of steampunk aesthetics and retro-futuristic design creates a captivating atmosphere unlike any other. From the moment you set foot in this realm, you'll feel as though you've been transported to another dimension.

One of the first technological wonders you'll encounter in Discoveryland is HyperSpace Mountain: Brace yourself for a thrilling adventure as you board your rocket and launch into the unknown. The twists, turns, and drops will leave you exhilarated and craving for more. Just remember to hold on tight and keep your eyes open – you wouldn't want to miss the breathtaking views of the cosmos.I

If you're in the mood for a more leisurely journey, hop aboard the Nautilus in Les Mystères du Nautilus. Inspired by Jules Verne's classic novel "20,000 Leagues Under the Sea," this immersive walkthrough attraction takes you deep beneath the waves in Captain Nemo's submarine. Marvel at the intricate details of the Nautilus, as you explore its various chambers and encounter mysterious creatures of the deep.

For those seeking an intergalactic adventure, look no further than Star Tours: The Adventures Continue. Join the Rebel Alliance on a thrilling 3D flight through the Star Wars galaxy, where you'll encounter iconic characters and visit legendary locations. With multiple storylines and destinations, no two rides are ever the same. Buckle up and get ready to embark on a journey that's out of this world!

But Discoveryland isn't just about heart-pounding thrills – it's also a place where you can satisfy your curiosity for the wonders of technology. Head over to Videopolis and witness the magic of the Animatronics. These lifelike robots will astound you with their realistic movements and expressions. It's a true testament to the incredible advancements in animatronic technology.

As you explore Discoveryland, be sure to keep an eye out for the hidden gems scattered throughout the area. From secret pathways to tucked-away shops, these hidden treasures add an extra layer of excitement to your adventure. And don't forget to refuel at one of the many dining options available.

Whether you're craving a quick bite or a sit-down meal, you'll find something to satisfy every palate.

As the day comes to a close, make sure to stick around for the spectacular nighttime shows and parades. From dazzling fireworks to enchanting light displays, these nighttime spectacles will leave you in awe. It's the perfect way to end your day of exploration in Discoveryland.

So, my fellow adventurers, get ready to embark on a journey of discovery like no other. Step into the futuristic world of Discoveryland and let your imagination run wild. From thrilling attractions to technological wonders, this is a place where dreams come true and the future is now.

Remember, the only limit is your imagination – and maybe a little bit of gravity!

CHAPTER 4

Hidden Gems

Here are some hidden gems and secrets of Disneyland Paris:

1. The story behind Phantom Manor: Phantom Manor, the Disneyland Paris version of the Haunted Mansion, has a unique backstory. The manor's owners, the Ravenswood family, were wealthy gold miners until they discovered a cursed treasure. Legend has it that the curse caused the family to suffer tragic deaths, leading to the haunting of the mansion.

2. The tribute to Walt Disney: On Main Street, USA, there is a window above the shops labeled "Storyteller" with a dedication to "Walter E. Disney, Esquire". This window pays tribute to Walt Disney, the founder of the Disneyland theme park.

3. The secret cast member room: In Adventureland, there is a door with a sign that reads "Cast Members Only". Behind the door is a small room where cast members can take a break and relax.

4. The hidden Pumbaa silhouette: In Adventureland, near the entrance of the Indiana Jones and the Temple of Peril ride, there is a silhouette of Pumbaa from The Lion King carved into a rock.

5. The restaurant with a view: At Walt Disney Studios Park, the Restaurant des Stars has an outdoor seating area with a view of the Twilight Zone Tower of Terror ride.

6. The walking tour of Sleeping Beauty's Castle: Disneyland Paris offers a guided tour of Sleeping Beauty's Castle, which takes visitors

through the story of the fairy tale.

7. The secret messages in Alice's Curious Labyrinth: In the maze at Fantasyland, there are hidden messages and quotes from Lewis Carroll's Alice's Adventures in Wonderland carved into the walls.

8. The easter egg in Toy Story Playland: At the Toy Story Playland, there is a sign for "Al's Toy Barn", a reference to the toy store in Toy Story 2.

9. The hidden Mickey Mouse silhouettes: Throughout the parks, there are hidden Mickey Mouse silhouettes, including on the wallpaper in the queue for the Crush's Coaster ride and in the design of the paving stones on Main Street, USA.

10. The insider tips from cast members: Disneyland Paris is home to a team of cast members who are always happy to share insider tips and information with visitors. Whether it's the best time to ride popular attractions or the best places to grab a snack, the cast members are a great resource for getting the most out of your visit to the park.

11. The dragon under the castle: Beneath Sleeping Beauty's Castle, there is a dark dungeon that houses a giant animatronic dragon. The dragon occasionally roars and breathes smoke, providing a thrilling experience for visitors.

12. The different ending for Pirates of the Caribbean: The Pirates of the Caribbean ride at Disneyland Paris has a different ending from the ride at other Disney parks. Instead of a battle scene between pirates and villagers, the ride ends with a peaceful scene of the pirates' loot and treasures.

13. The hidden Tarzan's Treehouse: In Adventureland, there is a hidden path that leads to Tarzan's Treehouse. The treehouse is a replica of the one seen in the Tarzan movie and features a rope bridge, slides, and interactive elements.

14. The tribute to Mary Poppins: On Main Street, USA, there is a shop called "Les Delices de Minnie" with a chimney that sports the same

shape and design as Mary Poppins' hat. This is a tribute to the classic movie.

15. The mysterious phone number: In Frontierland, there is an old-fashioned telephone booth that has a phone number printed on it. When visitors dial the number, they hear a pre-recorded message that tells the story of the Lucky Nugget Saloon, a restaurant in the area.

16. The secret Mickey and Minnie apartment: Above the Liberty Arcade on Main Street, USA, there is a small apartment that is decorated as Mickey and Minnie Mouse's living space. The apartment is only accessible by cast members and is used as a break room.

17. The hidden vault: In Adventureland, near the entrance of the Pirates of the Caribbean ride, there is a hidden vault with a door marked "Private". The door opens to reveal a secret room with treasure chests and pirate props.

18. The secret path to Fantasyland: In Discoveryland, there is a hidden pathway that leads to Fantasyland. The path is marked by a door with the phrase "To Infinity and Beyond" written in Aurebesh, the fictional language from the Star Wars series.

19. The hidden portrait in the Phantom Manor: In the Phantom Manor ride, there is a hidden portrait of a woman with a parasol. The portrait appears to change and reveal a skull when lightning strikes, adding to the ride's eerie atmosphere.

20. The hidden story in Alice's Tea Cups: The spinning tea cup ride in Fantasyland features teapots that have hidden names and labels, providing an additional layer of storytelling to the ride.

Character Meet and Greets

One of the most magical experiences at Disneyland Paris is the chance to meet and interact with your favourite Disney characters. Whether you're a lifelong fan of Mickey Mouse or have a soft spot for the princesses, these character meet and greets are not to be missed. But with long queues and limited time, it can be overwhelming to figure out the best way to make the most of these encounters.

That's why I'm here to share with you some tips for meeting beloved Disney characters in special locations and with shorter queues.

Tip 1: Be an Early Bird - If you want to beat the crowds and maximise your chances of meeting characters without a long wait, arrive at the park early. Most character meet and greets begin shortly after the park opens, so getting there early will give you a head start. Plus, there's something truly magical about being one of the first to greet your favourite characters as they start their day in the park.

Tip 2: Research the Special Locations - While character meet and greets can be found throughout the park, there are certain locations where you can meet specific characters in a more unique and immersive setting. For example, you can meet Cinderella and other princesses at the Princess Pavilion, located in Fantasyland. This charming location allows you to step into a fairytale and have a more intimate encounter with your favourite princesses. Similarly, you can find Mickey Mouse himself at the Meet Mickey Mouse theatre in Fantasyland. This is a must-visit spot where you can meet Mickey in a classic Disney setting.

Tip 3: Look out for Character Dining Experiences - If you want to combine a delicious meal with the opportunity to meet multiple characters, consider booking a character dining experience. These experiences take place at various restaurants throughout the park and offer a unique opportunity to interact with characters while enjoying a scrumptious meal. From breakfast with the princesses at Auberge de Cendrillon to a buffet-style lunch with Mickey and friends at Plaza Gardens Restaurant, these dining experiences are not only convenient but also provide a more relaxed and personal interaction with the characters.

Tip 4: Take Advantage of Premier Access - Just like with popular attractions, some character meet and greets offer Premier Access options. Premier Access allows you to reserve a specific time slot to meet your favourite characters, minimising your waiting time. This is especially useful for characters that tend to draw large crowds, such as Anna and Elsa from Frozen. Be sure to check the Disneyland Paris app or consult the park's schedule to see which character meet and greets offer Premier Access options and plan accordingly.

Tip 5: Keep an Eye on the Parade Routes - Did you know that characters often make appearances during the parades at Disneyland Paris? Keep an eye on the parade routes and try to position yourself near a character spot. This way, you can not only enjoy the magical spectacle of the parade but also have the chance to see your favourite characters up close. It's like getting a bonus meet and greet!

Now that you have these tips in your back pocket, you'll be well-prepared to navigate the world of character meet and greets at Disneyland Paris.

Remember to bring your autograph book, strike a pose, and most importantly, have fun! After all, these encounters are not just about the photos and autographs, but the lifelong memories they create.

So go ahead, embrace your inner child, and let the magic of Disneyland Paris bring your favourite characters to life.

Unique Dining Experiences

Themed restaurants and special dining experiences within

Disneyland Paris take the magic of the park to a whole new level. Whether you're a fan of Disney classics or looking for a culinary adventure, there's something for everyone to enjoy. From whimsical character dining to immersive themed restaurants, let's explore some recommendations for unique dining experiences in the happiest place on earth!

Auberge de Cendrillon:Step into a fairytale at Auberge de Cendrillon, a charming restaurant inspired by the beloved Cinderella story. As you enter the grand dining hall, you'll be greeted by Cinderella herself and other Disney princesses, ready to make your dining experience truly magical. Indulge in gourmet French cuisine while being entertained by live music and enchanting interactions with the princesses. Don't forget to try the pumpkin-inspired dishes for a truly immersive dining experience!

Captain Jack's - Le Restaurant des Pirates:Ahoy, mateys! If you're in the mood for a swashbuckling adventure, Captain Jack's - Le Restaurant des Pirates is the place to be. This immersive dining experience takes you into the world of pirates, with a stunningly designed restaurant that replicates an ancient grotto. Enjoy a hearty meal while being surrounded by pirate-themed décor, including treasure chests, cannons, and even a pirate ship! Keep an eye out for Captain Jack Sparrow himself, who may make a surprise appearance during your meal.

Ratatouille: The Adventure - The Restaurant:Step into the whimsical world of Pixar's Ratatouille at this unique dining experience. Located in the heart of the Walt Disney Studios Park, Ratatouille: The Adventure - The Restaurant invites you to Gusteau's restaurant, where you'll feel like a rat in Chef Remy's kitchen. The restaurant perfectly captures the charm and ambiance of the movie, with oversized food props and playful décor. Be prepared for a culinary delight as you savour French cuisine inspired by the film, including the famous ratatouille dish itself!

Victoria's Home-Style Restaurant:Travel back in time to Victorian England at Victoria's Home-Style Restaurant, nestled in Disneyland Hotel. This elegant and nostalgic dining experience takes you on a culinary journey through classic English cuisine. From traditional roasts to delectable desserts, each dish is prepared with love and attention to detail. The cozy atmosphere and impeccable service make this restaurant a must-visit for those seeking a refined dining experience.

So there you have it, a taste of the unique dining experiences that await you in Disneyland Paris. From fairy tales to pirate adventures and Pixar magic, each restaurant offers a one-of-a-kind dining experience that will leave you with unforgettable memories.

So go ahead, indulge in the magic and let your taste buds embark on an extraordinary culinary journey.
After all, in Disneyland Paris, even the dining experiences are out of this world!

And remember, if you're counting calories, don't worry, they're all Mickey-shaped, so they don't count!

Exclusive Merchandise

As you stroll through the whimsical streets of Disneyland Paris, with the magical castle towering above you, you can't help but feel like a kid in a candy store. And speaking of candy stores, there's one aspect of this enchanting realm that captures the hearts of Disney lovers around the world - exclusive merchandise.Now, I know what you're thinking.

"Exclusive merchandise? Isn't that just a fancy way of saying expensive souvenirs?"

Well, first-timers, prepare to have your minds blown. Exclusive merchandise is not just about splurging on trinkets and t-shirts; it's about finding the perfect memento to commemorate your visit to the happiest place on earth.So, how does one embark on the noble quest of finding these limited edition treasures? Fear not, for I shall be your guide through this retail wonderland.

First, let's talk about the art of the hunt. Just like a true adventurer, you need a plan. Start by visiting the official Disney shops scattered throughout the park. These magical emporiums are filled to the brim with unique items that can only be found within the boundaries of Disneyland Paris.

Now, I must warn you, my dear readers, the world of exclusive merchandise is a fickle one. The items you seek may not always be readily available. They may appear and disappear like a mischievous Cheshire cat.

But fret not, for I have a secret weapon up my sleeve - Disney Pin Trading. This delightful tradition allows you to trade pins with cast members and fellow enthusiasts, unlocking a whole new world of collectible goodies.But wait, there's more!

Did you know that Disneyland Paris hosts special events throughout the year, each with its own exclusive merchandise?

From Halloween spooktaculars to Christmas wonderlands, these events offer a treasure trove of limited edition goodies. So, keep an eye on the park's calendar and make sure to plan your visit accordingly.Now, I must confess, my fellow Disney enthusiasts, that I have a weakness for exclusive merchandise myself.

On my last visit, I stumbled upon a pair of Mickey Mouse ears adorned with the Pixar Elemental characters I couldn't resist the temptation, and I must say, they make my wife feel like a true Disney diva.

So, my advice to you is this - let your heart be your guide. If an item speaks to you, if it tugs at your heartstrings and makes your inner child leap with joy, then it's worth every penny.

Remember, it's not just about the item itself; it's about the memories and experiences it represents.So, my dear first-timers, as you embark on your journey through Disneyland Paris, don't forget to keep an eye out for exclusive merchandise. These elusive treasures are the cherry on top of your magical adventure.

Whether it's a limited edition pin, a special edition plush toy, or a one-of-a-kind piece of artwork, let these items be a tangible reminder of the joy and wonder you experienced within these hallowed grounds.

CHAPTER 5

Food and Drink

Quick Service Restaurants

When you're on the go and hunger strikes, there's nothing more satisfying than a quick service restaurant. These convenient dining options are designed for those moments when you need to refuel and get back to the excitement of Disneyland Paris. From delicious burgers to mouthwatering pizzas, quick service restaurants offer a variety of tasty options that are sure to please even the pickiest of eaters. Complete list of quick service restaurants at the bottom.

One of the great things about quick service restaurants is their accessibility. Located throughout the park, you won't have to wander too far to find one. Whether you're in Frontierland, Adventureland, or Fantasyland, there's a quick service restaurant nearby ready to satisfy your cravings.
Just follow your nose, and the tantalising smells of freshly cooked food will lead you right to them.
Now, let's talk about the food. Quick service restaurants offer a wide range of menu items, ensuring that there's something for everyone. If you're in the mood for a classic American meal, head on over to Casey's Corner on Main Street, U.S.A.

Indulge in a juicy hot dog, piled high with all your favourite toppings. And don't forget to try their famous corn dog nuggets – their the stuff dreams are made of.

If you're in the mood for something a little more adventurous, head to Hakuna Matata in Adventureland. This African-inspired quick service restaurant offers a variety of dishes that are bursting with flavour. From savoury couscous to tender grilled chicken, you'll feel like you've been transported straight to the heart of the African savannah.

And let's not forget about the pizza lovers out there. At Pizzeria Bella Notte in Fantasyland, you can indulge in a delicious slice of authentic Italian pizza. Made with fresh ingredients and baked to perfection, each bite is a taste of Italy. And if you're feeling extra hungry, why not try their pasta dishes? From spaghetti carbonara to lasagna, these mouthwatering options are sure to satisfy your cravings.But quick service restaurants aren't just about the food – they're about the experience too.

Many of these restaurants are themed to enhance your dining experience and immerse you in the world of Disney. From dining in a pirate ship at Captain Hook's Galley to enjoying a meal in the heart of a Wild West saloon at Cowboy Cookout Barbecue, the atmosphere adds an extra touch of magic to your meal.

Now, I know what you're thinking – what about the queues? Don't worry, Disneyland Paris has thought of that too. With mobile ordering available at select quick service restaurants, you can skip the line and order your meal in advance.
Just imagine the envy on the faces of those waiting in line as you stroll right past them, ready to collect your delicious food.

So, the next time you're exploring the wonders of Disneyland Paris and your stomach starts rumbling, remember the quick service restaurants. With their delicious food, convenient locations, and themed atmospheres, they're the perfect option for those meals on the go. Plus, with the added bonus of skipping the line with mobile ordering, you'll have more time to enjoy all the excitement that Disneyland Paris has to offer.

Here is a list of quick service restaurants in Disneyland Paris, along with a brief description of what they typically offer:

1. Colonel Hathi's Pizza Outpost (Adventureland): This restaurant serves a variety of pizzas, including classic options like Margherita and Pepperoni, as well as vegetarian and vegan choices.

2. Hakuna Matata Restaurant (Adventureland): Offering a selection of African-inspired dishes, this restaurant serves meals like rotisserie chicken, vegetable couscous, and refreshing fruit salads.

3. Toad Hall Restaurant (Fantasyland): This British-inspired eatery serves fish and chips, savoury pies, and other traditional English fare. It's a great spot for classic British comfort food.

4. Pizzeria Bella Notte (Fantasyland): Inspired by "Lady and the Tramp," this restaurant offers a range of Italian dishes, including pizza, pasta, and salads.

5. Au Chalet de la Marionnette (Fantasyland): Located near the "Pinocchio's Fantastic Journey" attraction, this quick-service eatery offers a selection of sandwiches, snacks, and refreshments.

6. Cowboy Cookout Barbecue (Frontierland): As the name suggests, this restaurant specialises in American-style barbecue. You can find dishes like ribs, chicken, cornbread, and coleslaw.

7. Last Chance Café (Frontierland): This Old West-themed restaurant serves Tex-Mex cuisine, including items like nachos, burritos, chilli, and salads.

8. Casey's Corner (Main Street, U.S.A.): This classic American-style eatery offers a variety of hot dogs, including specialty options like chilli cheese dogs and corn dog nuggets.

9. Market House Deli (Main Street, U.S.A.): Serving deli-style sandwiches, salads, and snacks, this spot is a good choice for a quick and satisfying meal.

10. Victoria's Home-Style Restaurant (Main Street, U.S.A.): Located inside Disneyland Hotel, this restaurant offers a selection of classic

American dishes, including burgers, sandwiches, and salads.

Please note that menu items and availability may vary, and it's always a good idea to check the official Disneyland Paris website or consult a park map for the most up-to-date information on dining options, menus, and operating hours.

Remember, good food and good fun go hand in hand. So, why wait? Head to a quick service restaurant and embark on a culinary adventure that will leave your taste buds and your heart happy.

Table Service Restaurants

When it comes to dining at Disneyland Paris, the options are as diverse as the attractions themselves. From fast food joints to fine dining establishments, there is something to satisfy every taste bud and budget. But if you're looking for a truly unforgettable dining experience, then look no further than the table service restaurants.These full-service restaurants not only offer a variety of cuisines, but also provide a unique dining experience that will make your trip to Disneyland Paris even more magical.

Whether you're in the mood for French cuisine, American classics, or exotic flavours from around the world, you're sure to find a table service restaurant that suits your palate.

One of the top recommendations for table service restaurants is Captain Jack's – Restaurant des Pirates. Located inside the Pirates of the Caribbean attraction, this restaurant offers a one-of-a-kind dining experience. Imagine enjoying a delicious meal while watching the boats float by on the attraction's gentle waters, with the sounds of swashbuckling adventures in the background. It's a true feast for the senses! The menu offers a fusion of flavours from around the world, with dishes inspired by Caribbean, Asian, and European cuisines. And be prepared for a few surprises along the way – you never know when a pirate might make an appearance!

For those craving a taste of France, Auberge de Cendrillon is a must-visit. This charming restaurant transports you to the fairytale world of Cinderella, with its medieval-style architecture and elegant decor. The menu features traditional French dishes, such as escargot and coq au vin, prepared with a touch of Disney magic.

The menu offers a fusion of flavours from around the world, with dishes inspired by Caribbean, Asian, and European cuisines. And be prepared for a few surprises along the way – you never know when a pirate might make an appearance!

For fans of American classics, the Walt's – An American Restaurant is a must-try. Located on Main Street, U.S.A., this restaurant pays homage to the man behind the magic – Walt Disney himself. The menu features all-American favourites, such as juicy burgers, crispy fried chicken, and mouthwatering milkshakes. And the best part?
You can enjoy your meal while taking in panoramic views of Main Street and the iconic Sleeping Beauty Castle.

Here is a list of table service restaurants in Disneyland Paris, along with a brief description of what they typically offer:

Auberge de Cendrillon (Fantasyland): Inspired by Cinderella's story, this restaurant offers a magical dining experience with a menu featuring French-inspired cuisine. You can enjoy dishes like grilled meats, seafood, and decadent desserts while meeting Disney Princesses.

Captain Jacks(Adventureland): Nestled within the Pirates of the Caribbean attraction, this unique restaurant immerses guests in a tropical Caribbean setting. The menu includes seafood dishes, grilled meats, and flavourful island-inspired specialties.

Plaza Gardens Restaurant (Main Street, U.S.A.): Located at the entrance of the park, this buffet-style restaurant offers a diverse range of international cuisines. You can enjoy a wide selection of dishes, including salads, meats, pasta, and desserts.

Silver Spur Steakhouse (Frontierland): This Western-themed steakhouse serves up delicious grilled meats, including various cuts of steak, ribs, and other hearty fare. It offers a hearty dining experience reminiscent of the Old West.

Hunter's Grill & Beaver Creek Tavern (Disney's Sequoia Lodge): Located in the Disney's Sequoia Lodge hotel, this restaurant offers a buffet-style dining experience. The menu includes a variety of dishes, including grilled meats, seafood, and vegetarian options.

Inventions (Disneyland Hotel): Set within the iconic Disneyland Hotel, Inventions offers a character dining experience where guests can enjoy a buffet meal while meeting beloved Disney characters. The menu features a wide range of dishes to suit different tastes. (Closed as of writing July 2023)

Walt's - An American Restaurant (Main Street, U.S.A.): This elegant restaurant pays tribute to Walt Disney's legacy. Each dining room represents a different era of Disneyland history, and the menu offers a refined selection of American cuisine.

Please note that menu offerings and availability may vary, and it's always a good idea to check the official Disneyland Paris website or consult a park map for the most up-to-date information on dining options, menus, and reservation requirements.

But it's not just about the food at these table service restaurants – it's also about the dining experience. From the moment you step foot inside, you'll be transported to a different world, where every detail is designed to enhance your meal. From the elegant decor to the attentive service, you'll feel like royalty from start to finish.

So, next time you're at Disneyland Paris, be sure to make a reservation at one of the table service restaurants., We personally use the app to book ahead as sometimes the restuarants are fully booked at least two months ahead.

Whether you're looking for a romantic dinner for two or a fun-filled feast with the whole family, these restaurants offer a dining experience that is truly unforgettable.

And remember, if you see a mouse in a chef's hat, don't worry – it's just Mickey Mouse trying out some new recipes!

Character Dining

One of the most enchanting experiences that Disneyland Paris has to offer is Character Dining. Imagine sitting down to enjoy a delicious meal, only to be joined by some of your favourite Disney characters! It's like having a personal meet-and-greet while enjoying scrumptious food – talk about a dream come true!

Character Dining is the perfect opportunity for guests to interact with beloved characters from classic Disney movies, including Mickey Mouse, Minnie Mouse, Donald Duck, and even the princesses like Cinderella and Belle. And let me tell you, these characters don't just stop by for a quick photo – they go above and beyond to create magical moments that you'll cherish forever.

But before you dive into this delightful experience, let's talk about how it all works. Character Dining is usually offered at select restaurants within the Disneyland Paris resort, and advanced reservations are highly recommended. Trust me, you don't want to miss out on this enchanting experience, so make sure to plan ahead and secure your spot at the dining table.

Once you're seated, get ready for a parade of characters to make their way to your table. They'll take turns visiting each table, posing for photos, signing autographs, and engaging in playful banter. It's a truly interactive experience that will leave you with a smile from ear to ear. And don't worry if you're too busy savouring your meal to grab a photo – Disney's PhotoPass photographers are there to capture all the magical moments for you.

Now, let's talk about the food.
The dining options at Character Dining are as diverse as the Disney characters themselves. From hearty buffets with a wide array of international cuisine to elegant table-service restaurants serving gourmet dishes, there's something to satisfy every palate. And of course, there are plenty of options for little ones too, with kid-friendly favourites like chicken nuggets and macaroni and cheese.

But here's a tip – don't be shy about indulging in your favourite treats. After all, you're in the most magical place on earth, so why not enjoy some Mickey-shaped waffles or a decadent dessert? Just make sure to save some room for the character-themed cupcakes and pastries – they're almost too cute to eat!

So, whether you're a die-hard Disney fan or simply looking for a unique and unforgettable dining experience, Character Dining is a must-do at Disneyland Paris.

It's the perfect way to combine delicious food with the joy of meeting your favourite Disney characters. Just be prepared for the laughter, the smiles, and the magical memories that will last a lifetime. Bon appétit and have a character-filled day!

Snacks and Treats

When it comes to indulging your taste buds, Disneyland Paris doesn't disappoint. From sweet to savoury, crunchy to creamy, the parks offer a wide array of snacks and treats that will have your mouth watering and your stomach growling in anticipation.Let's start with the classic Mickey Mouse-shaped treats that are practically synonymous with Disneyland. Whether it's a Mickey-shaped ice cream bar or a Mickey-shaped pretzel, these iconic snacks are a must-try for any Disney fan.

There's just something about biting into that familiar silhouette that makes the treat taste even better.If you're looking for something a little more whimsical, head over to the Cheshire Cat Café, where you'll find an assortment of fantastical treats inspired by Alice in Wonderland. From Cheshire Cat tail-shaped pastries to Mad Hatter-themed cupcakes, these treats are not only delicious but also visually stunning.Just be careful, they might just disappear before your very eyes!

But it's not all about the sweets at Disneyland Paris. There are also plenty of savoury snacks to satisfy your cravings.

Take a stroll through Adventureland and you'll come across the exotic flavours of the Hakuna Matata Snack Stand. Here, you can savour the taste of Africa with their flavourful samosas or sink your teeth into a juicy skewer of grilled chicken. It's a culinary adventure that will transport your taste buds to a whole new world.Of course, no trip to Disneyland Paris would be complete without sampling the famous French cuisine.

Luckily, the parks offer a variety of French-inspired snacks and treats that are sure to delight your palate. From buttery croissants to delicate macarons, these French delicacies are a taste of Paris in the heart of the magical kingdom.

The parks are filled with hidden gems and secret spots where you can find the most delicious treats that are often overlooked by the crowds.

So, whether you have a sweet tooth or a hankering for something savoury, Disneyland Paris has got you covered. From Mickey-shaped treats to French delicacies, there's a snack or treat for every palate. So go ahead, indulge your taste buds and treat yourself to a culinary adventure like no other.

After all, it's not every day you get to enjoy snacks and treats in the most magical place on earth!

And remember, calories don't count in Disneyland. It's a proven scientific fact (I think).

So go ahead, have that extra scoop of ice cream or that second helping of churros. You're on vacation, after all! Just be sure to take plenty of pictures of your delicious snacks and treats to make your friends back home jealous, and to post on your social feeds.

Special Dietary Needs

In a world filled with culinary delights, it's important to remember that not everyone's taste buds march to the same beat.

We all have our own dietary preferences and restrictions, and Disneyland Paris understands that. From gluten-free to vegan, lactose-intolerant to nut-free, they've got you covered with a plethora of options that will make your taste buds sing with joy.So, you may be wondering, how does one navigate the labyrinth of dining options at the happiest place on earth?

Fear not, my foodie friend, for I have some tips and tricks up my sleeve to ensure that your special dietary needs are met and exceeded.First and foremost, it's essential to plan ahead. Before embarking on your magical journey, take some time to research the various dining establishments in the park and surrounding areas. Disneyland Paris offers a wide range of restaurants that cater to different dietary needs, so you're bound to find something that tickles your fancy.

Once you've identified the dining options that suit your needs, it's time to make some reservations. Trust me, you don't want to be wandering around the park, stomach growling, desperately searching for a place to eat.

Make use of Disneyland Paris' online reservation system or call ahead to ensure that you have a table waiting for you.Now, let's talk about the actual dining experience. When you arrive at the restaurant, don't be shy about informing the staff about your dietary restrictions or preferences.

They are well-trained in accommodating various needs and will be more than happy to assist you.If you have specific dietary concerns, such as a severe nut allergy or gluten intolerance, it's always a good idea to speak directly to the chef.

They can provide you with detailed information about the ingredients used in each dish and even whip up something special just for you.But what about those moments when hunger strikes and you find yourself in need of a quick snack?

Fear not, for Disneyland Paris has you covered. They offer a wide range of grab-and-go options that cater to various dietary needs. From fresh fruit cups to gluten-free popcorn, you'll find something to satisfy your cravings.

Now, let's take a moment to address the elephant in the room - desserts.

We all know that no trip to Disneyland Paris is complete without indulging in a sweet treat or two. Luckily, they have a fantastic selection of desserts that cater to different dietary needs. Whether you're craving a vegan chocolate cake or a gluten-free apple tart, you can rest assured that Disneyland Paris has your dessert dreams covered.

As you embark on your culinary adventure through Disneyland Paris, keep in mind that the staff is there to assist you every step of the way.

Don't hesitate to ask questions, make special requests, or even crack a joke or two. After all, laughter is the best seasoning for any meal.

So, my foodie friend, embrace your special dietary needs and let Disneyland Paris dazzle your taste buds. From the first bite to the last, you'll be reminded that no matter your dietary restrictions or preferences, deliciousness knows no bounds at the happiest place on earth. Bon appétit!

CHAPTER 6

Parades and Shows

Daytime Parades

When the sun is high in the sky and the energy at Disneyland Paris is at its peak, it's time for the daytime parades to take centre stage. These lively and colourful processions bring the beloved Disney characters to life in a spectacle that will leave you awe-struck and smiling from ear to ear.

Picture this: a vibrant sea of people lining the streets, eagerly waiting for the parade to begin. The atmosphere is electric, filled with anticipation and excitement. And then, like magic, the first notes of a catchy tune fill the air, and the parade floats come into view.

The floats are a sight to behold, each one meticulously crafted and adorned with intricate details. From the sparkling costumes of the performers to the dazzling lights and special effects, no expense is spared to create a truly enchanting experience. You'll find yourself lost in a world where dreams come true and anything is possible.

As the floats make their way along the parade route, you'll be treated to a showcase of Disney's most beloved characters. Mickey and Minnie Mouse, Donald Duck, Goofy, and their friends will dance and wave to the crowd, their infectious energy contagious. The princesses will grace you with their elegance, while the villains will bring a touch of mischief and intrigue.

And of course, no parade would be complete without the lovable Disney Pixar characters, who will make you laugh and cheer along with their antics.But it's not just about the characters. The daytime parades at Disneyland Paris are a feast for the senses. The music will transport you to another world, with catchy tunes that will have you tapping your feet and singing along. The choreography is a work of art, with synchronised movements that showcase the talent and precision of the performers.

And let's not forget the confetti showers and bubble machines that add an extra touch of whimsy and fun.One of the highlights of the daytime parades is the interaction between the performers and the audience. You might find yourself being chosen to join in the fun, dancing alongside your favourite characters or even receiving a high-five from Mickey himself. These moments create memories that will last a lifetime, and you'll feel like a kid again, caught up in the magic of it all.

So, when planning your visit to Disneyland Paris, make sure to schedule some time for the daytime parades. They are a must-see spectacle that will captivate and entertain visitors of all ages. Whether you're a first-timer or a seasoned Disney enthusiast, the parades will leave you with a sense of wonder and joy that is truly unforgettable.And remember, if you're lucky enough to be chosen to participate in the parade, don't be afraid to let your inner child shine.

Nighttime Spectaculars

As the sun sets and the stars begin to twinkle in the sky, Disneyland Paris undergoes a magical transformation. It's a time when the park truly comes alive, casting its spell on all who are lucky enough to witness it. And at the heart of this enchantment are the nighttime spectaculars - the dazzling fireworks and breathtaking shows that illuminate the park and leave guests in awe.

Picture this: you're standing in the middle of Main Street, U.S.A, the iconic Sleeping Beauty Castle looming majestically ahead of you. The anticipation is palpable as the sky darkens, and then, without warning, a burst of light and colour fills the air. Fireworks explode in a symphony of sound and spectacle, painting the night sky with their brilliance. It's a sight that will take your breath away, leaving you spellbound and mesmerised. But it's not just the fireworks that make the nighttime spectaculars at Disneyland Paris so special, its the drones they deploy to create the amazing sequences and displays every night.

The park has a knack for combining pyrotechnics with storytelling, creating shows that transport you to another world. Whether it's the fantastical adventures of Mickey Mouse and his friends in "Disney Illuminations" or the timeless tale of the Lion King in "The Lion King: Rhythms of the Pride Lands," these shows are not just displays of pyrotechnic prowess, but immersive experiences that ignite your imagination.

One of the most beloved nighttime spectaculars is "Disney Dreams!," a show that celebrates the magic of Disney through a dazzling display of lights, water, and music. As you watch the castle transform into a canvas for animated projections, you'll be transported into the worlds of beloved Disney classics like "Beauty and the Beast," "The Little Mermaid," and "Aladdin."

It's a visual feast that will leave you feeling like a child again, full of wonder and delight.And let's not forget about the parades that take place under the cover of darkness. The nighttime parades at Disneyland Paris are a sight to behold, with floats adorned with thousands of twinkling lights and characters dancing their way down the streets.

From the classic "Disney Stars on Parade" to the spooktacular "Mickey's Halloween Celebration," these parades are a feast for the eyes and a celebration of all things Disney.But the magic of the nighttime spectaculars doesn't end with the shows themselves. Disneyland Paris has thought of every detail to make sure your experience is truly unforgettable. From special viewing areas that offer the best vantage points to the whimsical music that accompanies each show, every aspect is carefully crafted to transport you to a world of pure imagination.

So, whether you're a first-timer or a seasoned Disney enthusiast, make sure you don't miss out on the nighttime spectaculars at Disneyland Paris. It's a truly awe-inspiring experience that will leave you with memories to last a lifetime.

Seasonal Entertainment

As the seasons change, so does the entertainment at Disneyland Paris. Throughout the year, this magical park offers a variety of special performances and events that are sure to leave visitors in awe. From festive parades to enchanting night time shows, Disneyland Paris knows how to put on a show no matter the time of year.

One of the most anticipated seasonal events at Disneyland Paris is the Christmas season. As the air becomes crisp and the lights twinkle, the park transforms into a winter wonderland. Main Street is adorned with garlands and ornaments, and a giant Christmas tree takes centre stage in Town Square. The Christmas parade is a must-see, with Mickey and his friends dressed in their holiday best as they glide down the streets on dazzling floats. And let's not forget about the nightly fireworks show, where the sky is illuminated with bursts of colour and holiday cheer.

In the springtime, Disneyland Paris welcomes the arrival of the vibrant and whimsical Spring Festival. This is the perfect time to take a stroll through the beautifully manicured gardens and admire the blooming flowers. Be sure to catch the Spring Parade, where characters like Alice in Wonderland and the Mad Hatter dance and sing their way through the park. And for a truly immersive experience, don't miss the Spring Night-time Spectacular, where projections and fireworks light up Sleeping Beauty Castle in a dazzling display of springtime magic.Summer at Disneyland Paris means it's time for the Festival of the Lion King and Jungle season.

This exciting event brings the African savannah to life with energetic shows and interactive experiences. Join Timon and Pumbaa as they teach you the art of the Hakuna Matata dance, or venture into the depths of the jungle on the Indiana Jones and the Temple of Peril ride. And of course, no summer festival would be complete without a vibrant parade and a spectacular firework finale.

But perhaps the most enchanting time of year at Disneyland Paris is the Halloween season. As the leaves begin to fall, the park takes on a spooky and magical atmosphere. The Halloween Parade is a sight to behold, with Disney villains and characters dressed in their most wicked costumes. And when the sun sets, the Halloween Night-time Spectacular lights up the sky with eerie projections and bone-chilling fireworks. It's a hauntingly beautiful experience that is sure to send shivers down your spine.No matter the season, Disneyland Paris offers a year-round extravaganza of entertainment.

From the festive charm of Christmas to the whimsy of spring, there's always something special happening at this enchanting park.

Finding the Best Viewing Spots

When it comes to parades and shows at Disneyland Paris, finding the best viewing spots can feel like a competitive sport. But fear not, fellow Disneyland adventurers! I'm here to share with you some top-notch tips for securing prime locations to enjoy all the magical spectacles that await you.First things first, timing is everything. If you want to snag a front-row spot for the parade or show, you'll need to plan your day accordingly.

Arriving early is key. I'm talking "set-your-alarm-and-beat-the-crowds" kind of early. Trust me, it's worth it. By staking your claim early, you'll have your pick of the litter when it comes to viewing spots.

Now, let's talk strategy. Main Street, U.S.A. is a popular spot for parades, but it fills up quickly. So, why not venture off the beaten path? Consider exploring some of the less crowded areas, like Frontierland or Fantasyland, where you might find hidden gems of prime viewing spots. Plus, these areas offer a unique perspective on the parades and shows, giving you a fresh take on the magic.

Another pro tip: scout out the parade route ahead of time. Take a stroll along the parade route earlier in the day to scope out the best vantage points. Look for areas with fewer obstructions, like trees or lamp posts, that might hinder your view. And don't forget to take note of any benches or ledges that could double as impromptu seating. Your tired feet will thank you!

Now, let's get a little sneaky, shall we?
If you want a prime viewing spot without the hassle of camping out hours in advance, consider dining at a restaurant with a view.

Several restaurants in the park offer dining packages that include reserved seating for parades and shows. It's like getting the best of both worlds - a delicious meal and an amazing view. Talk about a win-win!

And here's a little secret for you: the best viewing spots for nighttime shows aren't always where you might expect. Sure, the hub in front of Sleeping Beauty Castle is a classic choice, but think outside the box.

Head over to Adventureland or Discoveryland for a unique perspective on the nighttime magic. You might just stumble upon a hidden spot that feels like your own private viewing party.

Oh, and one last thing. Don't forget to bring snacks and drinks to keep you fuelled and hydrated during the parade or show. Trust me, the excitement can work up quite an appetite.

Plus, it's always fun to enjoy a Mickey-shaped treat while taking in all the wonder.

So there you have it, my friends. With these tips in your pocket, you'll be well-equipped to find the best viewing spots at Disneyland Paris. Remember, timing, strategy, and a little bit of sneaky manoeuvring are your best friends.

CHAPTER 7

Practical Tips

Premier Access and Rider Switch

Premier Access and Rider Switch: The Keys to Conquering Disneyland ParisPicture this: you're standing in line for the most exhilarating roller coaster in all of Disneyland Paris. The anticipation is building, the excitement palpable. But then, it hits you like a ton of bricks - the line stretches out before you like an endless maze of frustration.

Fear not, my fellow adventurers, for I am here to unveil the secret weapons in your arsenal: Premier Access and Rider Switch.

Let's start with the Premier Access system, the ultimate VIP pass to skipping those dreaded lines. This ingenious creation allows you to reserve a specific time slot for select attractions, granting you access to a magical express lane that bypasses the hordes of eager visitors. It's like having a golden ticket to the chocolate factory, but instead of candy, you get to experience the most thrilling rides without the interminable wait.

Here's how it works: upon entering the park, locate a Premier Access distribution point near the attraction of your choice. Insert your park ticket into the machine, and voila! You receive a Premier Access with a designated return time window. But beware, my friends, these coveted passes are in high demand. The early bird catches the worm, or in this case, the Premier Passes. So be sure to snag them as soon as the park gates swing open, for they are limited in quantity.

Now, let's talk strategy. Premier Access
It's essential to plan your day strategically, like a chess grandmaster plotting their next move. Prioritise the attractions with the longest wait times and secure your Premier Access accordingly. Keep in mind that you can only hold one FastPass at a time, so choose wisely.

Once you've redeemed your Premier Access you can head back to another distribution point and grab another, like a never-ending loop of joyous skipping through the park. But wait, there's more! Now you can add the Premier Access pass to your app which makes scanning the QR code at ride entrances so much easier, and when booking your park tickets or hotel stays you can again add them in advance at the same time. At the time of writing there are two available choices:
Disney Premier Access Ultimate:
Use 1 time on each available attraction
Join the fast lane whenever you want - no time slots.
Buy in advance or on the day

The other option is Disney Premier Access One : Use 1 time on 1 attraction
Be allocated the next available time slot to join the fast lane
Buy on the day, in the Disney Parks
Buy via the Disneyland Paris app
Check on the official Disneyland Paris website for all up-to-date information and booking details.

Allow me to introduce you to Rider Switch, the ultimate ally for families with young children. We all know that little ones can't always ride the big, bad roller coasters, but that shouldn't dampen their Disney experience.

Enter Rider Switch, a marvel of modern family-friendly technology.Here's how it works: if you have a child who doesn't meet the height requirement for a particular attraction, one adult can wait in line while the other stays back with the young adventurer. Once the first adult has experienced the thrill of the ride, they can then switch places, allowing the second adult to enjoy the attraction without starting from square one. It's like having your own personal time-travel device, granting you the power to conquer every ride while ensuring no one misses out on the magic.

Now, for some tips and tricks to maximise your Premier Access and Rider Switch experience. First and foremost, timing is everything. Be sure to arrive at the park early to secure those coveted Premier Access passes before they disappear faster than Cinderella's glass slipper. Additionally, familiarise yourself with the Premier Access distribution locations for each attraction, saving precious time and energy.

Finally, don't forget to keep a keen eye out for those hidden gems - the attractions that often go overlooked but hold a charm all their own. While everyone else is sprinting to the big-name rides, you can take a leisurely stroll through the whimsical lands, exploring the enchanting nooks and crannies that make Disneyland Paris truly magical.

Photography and Memory Making

Tips for Capturing Memorable Photos and Creating Lasting Memories at Disneyland ParisWhen it comes to capturing the magic of Disneyland Paris, photography plays a crucial role. Whether you're a seasoned photographer or just someone armed with a smartphone, these tips will help you capture the most memorable moments and create lasting memories.

1. Timing is everything: The early bird catches the worm, and the early photographer catches the best shots. Arrive at the park early to avoid the crowds and get those picture-perfect moments without distractions. Plus, the morning light is often softer and more flattering, adding an ethereal glow to your photos.

2. Scout the locations: Disneyland Paris is a vast wonderland filled with hidden gems waiting to be discovered. Take some time to explore the park and find the best spots for your photos. From iconic landmarks like Sleeping Beauty Castle to lesser-known corners like the Alice's Curious Labyrinth, there are plenty of picturesque settings to choose from.

3. Embrace the magic hour: The magic hour, also known as the golden hour, refers to the period shortly after sunrise or before sunset when the lighting conditions are at their best. The warm, soft light during this time can transform even the most ordinary scene into something truly enchanting. Plan your photo sessions accordingly to make the most of this magical lighting.

4. Capture the details: Disneyland Paris is a treasure trove of intricate details that add depth and charm to your photos. Look beyond the grand vistas and focus on the little things that make the park unique. From the whimsical architecture to the colourful costumes worn by the characters, these small details can bring your photos to life and transport you back to the magical world of Disney.

5. Include people in your shots: While Disneyland Paris is undoubtedly a place of wonder, it's the people who bring it to life. Don't be afraid to include fellow visitors in your photos. Whether it's capturing the joy on a child's face or the awe in someone's eyes, these candid moments add a human touch to your memories and make your photos more relatable.

6. Experiment with angles and perspectives: Don't be afraid

to get creative with your photography. Try different angles, perspectives, and compositions to add a unique touch to your photos. Get down low to capture the grandeur of the castle or shoot from above to showcase the bustling crowds. Play around with different techniques and let your imagination run wild.

7. Capture the emotions: Disneyland Paris is a place where dreams come true, and emotions run high. Whether it's the excitement of meeting your favourite character or the sheer joy of experiencing a thrilling ride, try to capture these emotions in your photos. Candid shots of laughter, tears of joy, and wide-eyed wonder will bring back the memories and emotions long after your visit.

8. Don't forget the night-time magic: As the sun sets and the park transforms into a twinkling wonderland, don't put your camera away just yet.

Night-time at Disneyland Paris offers a whole new world of photographic opportunities. From the mesmerising light shows to the beautifully illuminated attractions, capturing the night-time magic will add an extra layer of enchantment to your memories.Remember, while capturing the perfect shot is important, don't let it consume your entire experience.

Take the time to put your camera down, immerse yourself in the magic, and create memories that go beyond what can be captured on film. After all, the best memories are the ones etched in our hearts, not just on our memory cards.So, grab your camera, unleash your inner child, and embark on a magical journey through the lens.

And remember, even if your photos don't turn out exactly as planned, the joy and laughter that accompany them are worth a thousand perfectly framed shots.

Happy memory making at Disneyland Paris!

Staying Comfortable

When visiting Disneyland Paris, it's important to dress comfortably and be prepared for a day filled with excitement and exploration.

Here is some advice on what to wear and what to take with you:

Comfortable Clothing: Opt for clothing that allows for ease of movement and comfort throughout the day. Choose breathable fabrics and dress in layers to accommodate changes in temperature. Consider wearing comfortable walking shoes as you'll be spending a lot of time on your feet.

Weather Considerations: Check the weather forecast before your visit to Disneyland Paris. Pack accordingly with items like a light jacket, raincoat, or umbrella in case of inclement weather. Don't forget to apply sunscreen and wear a hat to protect yourself from the sun on sunny days.

Practical Bags or Backpacks: Bring a small backpack or a bag that can securely hold your essentials. This will allow you to carry items like a refillable water bottle, snacks, sunscreen, sunglasses, a portable phone charger, and a map or guidebook.

Disney-themed Clothing or Accessories: Embrace the Disney spirit and consider wearing clothing or accessories that showcase your favourite Disney characters or represent the magical ambiance of the park. It adds to the fun and creates memorable photo opportunities.

Comfortable Accessories: Consider bringing a lightweight and comfortable crossbody bag or a fanny pack to keep your belongings easily accessible and secure. This frees up your hands for enjoying attractions and experiences without worrying about your possessions.

Practical Essentials: Don't forget to bring essentials like a valid ID, cash or credit cards, any necessary medications, and your mobile phone. It's also a good idea to have a printed or digital copy of your tickets or passes for entry.

Extra Clothing and Rain Gear: If you plan on experiencing water-based attractions or if there's a chance of rain, consider bringing a change of clothes or a poncho to keep yourself dry and comfortable throughout the day.

Comfortable clothing and shoes are a must for walking around the park, wearing loose fitting, and breathable clothing is also highly recommended.

Be prepared for the climate you're visiting in. Autumn and spring can have high chances of rain. Winter can be quite cold, so pack gloves, a hat and a warm coat. Summers can get very hot and sunny, so don't forget sun protection such as a hat, shades, sunblock, and plenty of water bottles.

When it comes to park policies, take note that bags are not allowed on some attractions, so plan to leave larger bags and personal belongings at your hotel room lockers or any public storage facilities Disneyland Paris provides for a small fee.

It's also worth packing a phone charger, some cash or credit/debit card, and an ID for any purchases, as well as an autograph book for meeting characters and some small souvenirs for the trip home.

Remember to be flexible with your planning and expectations when visiting Disneyland Paris, as the park may be busier than anticipated or closures may happen due to circumstances beyond Disney's control like weather issues, maintenance requirements, etc.

Remember, being prepared and dressing appropriately for the weather and activities will ensure a more enjoyable and stress-free experience at Disneyland Paris.

CHAPTER 8

Travelling With Children

Traveling to Disneyland Paris with children can be an incredibly exciting and memorable experience. As with any trip, planning ahead and being aware of the specific needs of your children can make all the difference in maximising the fun and minimising stress. Here are some tips and advice for families traveling to Disneyland Paris with children.

1. Attractions for children: Disneyland Paris offers many attractions aimed at younger visitors, including a range of rides, shows and parades that children will love. Make sure to visit Fantasyland, where classic Disney attractions such as "it's a small world," "Peter Pan's Flight," and "Dumbo the Flying Elephant" are located. Toy Story Land, opened in 2010, is also a must-visit area with its interactive games and Buzz Lightyear Laser Blast ride.

2. Meeting Disney Characters: One of the most exciting things for children visiting Disneyland Paris is the opportunity to meet their favourite Disney characters. From Mickey Mouse and Minnie Mouse to Buzz Lightyear and Cinderella, children will be delighted to see their favourite characters in person. Be sure to check the park schedule for character meet and greet times and locations, as these tend to change regularly.

3. Dining options: Disneyland Paris offers a range of dining options that cater to families with children. Buffet restaurants such as the Plaza Gardens and the Agrabah Café offer a wide range of dishes that

appeal to children's tastes, while table-service restaurants such as the Chez Remy and the Blue Lagoon Restaurant offer themed dining experiences that will be sure to captivate them. Snack options such as ice cream, popcorn and candy floss are also available throughout the park.

4. Toilets and baby-changing facilities: Disneyland Paris recognises that families with small children require convenient access to baby-changing facilities and toilets. Most toilets feature baby-changing stations, and there are several baby centers located within the park, such as Spyglass Inn and the Baby Care Center in Main Street USA.

5. Stroller rental: For parents with young children, bringing a stroller can be a lifesaver. However, bringing your own stroller can be a hassle. Fortunately, Disneyland Paris offers stroller rentals near the entrance gates, which can save you both time and hassle. The strollers are comfortable and easy to use, and you will be able to rent them for single or multiple days.

6. Premier Access and Rider Switch options: Disneyland Paris offers both Premier Access and Rider Switch options for its popular attractions. The Premier Access system allows you to skip the regular queue for an attraction by getting a time slot for a specific ride in advance, while Rider Switch enables a parent to wait outside an attraction with a child who is too young or scared to go on, while the other parent or adult goes on the ride. This ensures that both parents can enjoy popular attractions without sacrificing time away from their children.

7. Age-appropriate activities: Disneyland Paris is perfect for children of all ages. Be sure to tailor your activities to your children's ages, with older children enjoying thrilling rides such as Space Mountain, while younger children may enjoy the more gentle rides in Fantasyland. Parent-child activities such as the "Pirates of the Caribbean" boat ride are excellent choices for family bonding time & remember to smile for the camera.

Disneyland Paris is a magical destination for families with children.

With its fantastic lineup of attractions, dining options, and amenities tailored specifically to children, it is no wonder that it is a favourite family vacation destination.

By following the tips above, you can ensure that your family trip to Disneyland Paris will be unforgettable for all the right reasons.

Disney Village

Disney Village: While not part of the Walt Disney Studios park itself, the adjacent Disney Village offers a variety of dining, shopping, and entertainment options. It's a lively district with themed restaurants, live music venues, and a cinema complex, providing additional experiences for guests to enjoy after their visit to the park.

Here's a write-up for a first-timer's guide to Disney Village:

Disney Village is a vibrant and lively district adjacent to the Disneyland Paris parks, offering a plethora of dining, shopping, and entertainment options. As a first-time visitor, Disney Village provides a fantastic opportunity to extend the magic of your Disneyland Paris experience. Here's a guide to help you make the most of your time at Disney Village:

1. Dining Experiences:
Disney Village is home to a wide range of dining options, catering to various tastes and preferences. Whether you're in the mood for a quick bite or a leisurely meal, you'll find something to satisfy your cravings. From themed restaurants like Rainforest Cafe and Planet Hollywood (Now Closed) to family-friendly spots like Annette's Diner and Earl of Sandwich, there's a dining experience for every palate.

2. Shopping:
Explore the myriad of shops at Disney Village, where you'll find a treasure trove of Disney merchandise, fashion, accessories, and more.

The World of Disney store is a must-visit, offering a vast selection of Disney-themed items, from plush toys and apparel to collectibles and souvenirs. The LEGO Store, Disney Fashion, and Disney & Co. are also popular destinations for unique Disney merchandise.

3. Entertainment:
Disney Village comes alive with exciting entertainment options that are perfect for the whole family. Catch a movie at Gaumont Cinema, featuring the latest blockbusters. The Buffalo Bill's Wild West Show offers a thrilling dinner show experience with live action, horsemanship, and a delicious Tex-Mex feast. You can also enjoy live music and performances at venues like Billy Bob's Country Western Saloon.

4. Events and Special Occasions:
Disney Village often hosts special events throughout the year, including seasonal celebrations, live performances, and fireworks displays. Keep an eye on the Disneyland Paris website or ask at the information desk for details on any upcoming events during your visit. These events add an extra layer of excitement and magic to your experience.

5. Atmosphere and Ambiance:
Immerse yourself in the vibrant atmosphere of Disney Village. The streets are filled with music, lights, and a lively atmosphere, creating a sense of fun and entertainment. Take a leisurely stroll along the charming promenade, soak in the lively ambiance, and marvel at the picturesque scenery. It's a great place to relax, unwind, and soak up the Disney magic outside of the theme parks.

Disney Village at Disneyland Paris offers a variety of dining options to cater to different tastes and preferences. Here are some of the food places you can find at Disney Village:

Rainforest Cafe: This immersive restaurant transports guests into a lush tropical rainforest, complete with animatronic animals and themed decorations. The menu features a range of international cuisine, including burgers, pastas, salads, and seafood dishes.

Billy Bob's Country Western Saloon: La Grange Restaurant: Throw on your Stetson, grab a beer and prepare for a rootin' tootin' time in this authentic Wild West saloon and concert hall. If it's a Wild West feast you're after then Billy Bob's Country Western Saloon is the place for you. Cowboys and cowgirls can lasso a hearty plate of barbecue ribs, chicken wings, chilli con carne and more from the Tex-Mex-style buffet, before letting loose and strutting to some live music rocking from the bar below.

New York Style Sandwiches: Show-stopping Subs: Drop into this deli straight out of the streets of Manhattan for some hot and cold sandwiches and refreshing salads. Pick up some hot, cold, fresh paninis, pizzas and baguettes to enjoy on the move. Or sit in, enjoy the salad bar and admire the Broadway memorabilia that lines the mirrored walls of this New York-style sandwich shop.

Earl of Sandwich: As the name suggests, this eatery specialises in gourmet sandwiches. From hot sandwiches like the Original 1762 (roast beef, cheddar, and horseradish sauce) to cold options like the Caprese (mozzarella, tomatoes, and pesto), there's a sandwich for everyone's taste.

Five Guys: Known for its handcrafted burgers and fresh-cut fries, Five Guys is a popular fast-food spot at Disney Village. They offer a variety of burger options, including vegetarian and vegan choices, along with a range of toppings and milkshake flavours.

McDonald's: For those looking for a quick and familiar option, McDonald's is conveniently located in Disney Village. It serves the classic fast-food menu, including burgers, chicken nuggets, fries, and desserts.

Annette's Diner: Step back in time at this classic 1950s-style American diner. The menu features burgers, hot dogs, milkshakes, and other diner favourites. Guests can even enjoy a car-side dining experience with roller-skating waiters.

The Steakhouse: This restaurant offers a selection of grilled meats, including steaks, ribs, and poultry dishes. It provides a cozy atmosphere and hearty meals for meat lovers.

Starbucks: Coffee enthusiasts can grab their favourite caffeinated beverages and snacks at the Disney Village Starbucks location. It's a perfect spot for a quick pick-me-up.

Whether you're looking for dining experiences, shopping for Disney souvenirs, enjoying live entertainment, or simply taking in the unique atmosphere, Disney Village offers a delightful extension to your Disneyland Paris adventure.

It's a place where the magic continues outside the park gates, ensuring that your visit is filled with unforgettable experiences and cherished memories.

Please note that dining options and menus may vary, and it's always a good idea to check the official Disneyland Paris website or consult a map of Disney Village for the most up-to-date information on available food places, operating hours, and menu offerings.

CHAPTER 9

Walt Disney Studios

Walt Disney Studios at Disneyland Paris is a captivating park that celebrates the magic of cinema and the art of storytelling. As a first-time visitor, it's essential to make the most of your experience and explore the park's unique offerings. Here's a guide to help you navigate the wonders of Walt Disney Studios.

Here's a brief overview of the history and construction of the Walt Disney Studios at Disneyland Paris:

The Walt Disney Studios theme park at Disneyland Paris opened its doors on March 16, 2002, as part of the larger Disneyland Paris Resort. It was the second theme park to be built at the resort, complementing the original Disneyland Park.

The concept for the Walt Disney Studios originated from the success of the Disney-MGM Studios (now Disney's Hollywood Studios) in Walt Disney World, Florida. The idea was to create a park dedicated to the magic of movies, allowing guests to experience the behind-the-scenes world of filmmaking while also enjoying thrilling attractions and entertainment.

Construction on the Walt Disney Studios began in 2000, with Imagineers and designers meticulously crafting the park's layout and thematic areas. The park was designed to resemble a real working film studio, with themed backlots, sound-stages, and production facilities.

The park is divided into four main studio lots: Front Lot, Production

Courtyard, Backlot, and Toon Studio. Each area offers its own unique attractions and experiences, showcasing different aspects of the entertainment industry.

Throughout the years, the Walt Disney Studios has undergone expansions and additions to enhance the guest experience. Notable additions include the Toy Story Playland, inspired by the beloved Pixar films, and the Ratatouille: The Adventure attraction, which immerses guests in the world of the animated film.

The park continues to evolve, with ongoing development and the introduction of new experiences. It remains a hub of creativity and entertainment, capturing the magic and excitement of the cinematic world.

Today, the Walt Disney Studios stands as a celebration of the art of filmmaking, offering guests a chance to step into the world of movies, explore the secrets of special effects, and enjoy thrilling attractions inspired by beloved Disney and Pixar films.

It is a place where dreams and imagination come to life, making it a must-visit destination for movie enthusiasts and Disney fans alike.

Food at the Walt Disney Studios

Here is a list of restaurants at the Walt Disney Studios at Disneyland Paris, along with a brief description of each and a sample of what you can find on their menus:

Bistrot Chez Rémy: Step into Gusteau's restaurant from the film "Ratatouille" and enjoy French cuisine with a Ratatouille twist. The menu features dishes such as Ratatouille, Grilled Entrecote Steak, and Lemon Meringue Tart.

Café des Cascadeurs: This quick-service eatery offers a range of fast-food options, including burgers, sandwiches, and salads. The menu includes items like BBQ Bacon Cheeseburger, Chicken Caesar Salad, and a Vegetarian Burger.

Restaurant En Coulisse: Located in the Production Courtyard area, this buffet-style restaurant offers a variety of international dishes. The menu includes options such as roasted meats, pasta, salads, and a selection of desserts.

Studio Catering Co.: This counter-service restaurant offers a selection of sandwiches, salads, and snacks. The menu includes items like Chicken Caesar Wrap, Vegetable Couscous Salad, and a variety of desserts and beverages.

Les Stars'n'Cars Café: Located near the entrance of the park, this café offers a range of sandwiches, salads, and pastries. It's a convenient spot for a quick bite or a coffee break.

Le Comptoir de Rémy: Adjacent to the Ratatouille: The Adventure attraction, this kiosk serves grab-and-go snacks such as sandwiches, pastries, and drinks

Pym's Kitchen:This is a buffet restaurant that is themed of Ant Man. As such you can get unusually sized food as atman has used his Pym particle technology to grown and shrink foods. Theming and Decor: Formerly an assembly line for Howard Stark, it features relics of S.H.I.E.L.D.'s earlier activities and hosts many "Easter Eggs" hidden as fan tributes including artefacts built by Tony Stark and the impressive **HulkBuster** – the armour he created with the help of Bruce Banner for the Hulk, which is exclusive to Disneyland Paris.

Stark Factory: is a quick service restaurant where recruits refuelling will get to enjoy a cooking show experience with homemade pizzas fresh from the pizzaiolo oven.

Please note that menus and offerings may vary, and it's always a good idea to check the official Disneyland Paris website or consult a park map for the most up-to-date information on dining options, menus, and operating hours at the Walt Disney Studios.

Rides and Attractions

Ratatouille: The Adventure: Shrink down to the size of a rat and embark on a thrilling 3D dark ride through Gusteau's restaurant. This attraction combines dazzling special effects and immersive storytelling, making it a must-visit experience.

The Twilight Zone Tower of Terror: Plunge into the depths of the eerie Hollywood Tower Hotel aboard a haunted elevator. This exhilarating drop tower ride provides an adrenaline-pumping experience with its unpredictable drops and spine-chilling storyline.

Crush's Coaster: Join Crush, the sea turtle from "Finding Nemo," on a spinning roller coaster adventure through the East Australian Current. This unique attraction combines spinning vehicles, immersive theming, and thrilling twists and turns.

Toy Story Playland: Step into the world of Andy's backyard and enjoy family-friendly attractions like RC Racer, Slinky Dog Zigzag Spin, and Toy Soldiers Parachute Drop. These fun-filled rides capture the playful spirit of the beloved Toy Story films.

Hidden Features and Details:

Art of Disney Animation: Discover the magic of animation and learn about the artistry behind your favourite Disney characters. Explore interactive exhibits, watch animated film clips, and even learn to draw a Disney character from a Disney artist.

Hollywood Boulevard: The entrance area of the park, known as Hollywood Boulevard, is inspired by the iconic Hollywood Boulevard in Los Angeles. It features classic Hollywood architecture, a Walk of Fame with stars honoring Disney legends, and a charming atmosphere reminiscent of the golden age of cinema.

Avengers Campus

The Avengers Campus is a brand new land at Disneyland Paris' Walt

Disney Studios Park, which is dedicated to the Marvel Cinematic Universe and opened on July 20, 2022.

The highlight of the campus is the Avengers Headquarters building, where visitors can go on an action-packed rollercoaster ride and team up with Iron Man and Captain Marvel.

At the Avengers Campus at Disneyland Paris' Walt Disney Studios Park , visitors can meet various Marvel characters such as Iron Man, Captain Marvel, Black Panther, Doctor Strange, Spider-Man, and Ant-Man and The Wasp.

Join the mission for Avengers Assemble: Flight Force, a thrilling roller coaster that launches you 0-60 mph in less than 3 seconds! This ride will also feature the first Marvel Audio-Animatronic in a Disney Park as Iron Man greets you in his Mark 80 suit.

At the Avengers Campus at Disneyland Paris' Walt Disney Studios Park , visitors can meet various Marvel characters such as Iron Man, Captain Marvel, Black Panther, Doctor Strange, Spider-Man, and Ant-Man and The Wasp.

There are also two new Marvel-themed rides : "Avengers Assemble: Flight Force," a simulator ride where visitors team up with the Avengers to help them save the earth, and "WEB SLINGERS: A Spider-Man Adventure," an interactive ride where visitors help Spider-Man trap rogue Spider-Bots. Visitors can expect to experience thrilling effects, immersive environments, and action-packed scenes on both rides.

Beyond The Park

Here are some recommendations for off-site attractions that visitors can explore when they have extra time beyond the Disneyland Paris parks:

1. Paris: Disneyland Paris is located just 20 miles east of Paris, making it an perfect base for visitors wishing to explore the French capital.

Visitors can take a train, which can be reached in minutes from the park, to the city centre and indulge in a range of cultural and historical experiences including the Eiffel Tower, Arc de Triomphe, Notre-Dame Cathedral, the Louvre Museum and many other world-famous landmarks.

2. Versailles: The Palace of Versailles is only 48 minutes away from Disneyland Paris via train and is one of the most famous cultural sites in France. Visitors can experience the grandeur of the palace's opulent rooms, explore its manicured gardens and learn about its rich history as the former residence of the French monarchy.

3. Fontainebleau: Located about 45 minutes south of Disneyland Paris, the historic town of Fontainebleau is known for its picturesque forest and palace. The Fontainebleau Palace is a UNESCO World Heritage Site that served as the royal residence for several French monarchs and is known for its grand architecture and elaborate interior decoration.

4. Reims: Around 90 minutes from Disneyland Paris by car or train, Reims is an ancient city located in the Champagne region of France. It boasts an incredible cathedral – the Notre-Dame de Reims – which has a rich history dating back to the Roman Empire. Visitors can also tour the nearby Champagne cellars and indulge in some of the finest sparkling wines in the world.

5. Val d'Europe and La Vallée Village: Located only 10 minutes from Disneyland Paris, these two shopping destinations offer a mix of luxury and outlet shopping, and are perfect for those who enjoy retail therapy. Val d'Europe features more than 100 stores, such as Zara, Gap, and Lego store, while La Vallée Village offers many luxury brands such as Armani, Gucci, and Michael Kors at discounted prices.

6. Beauvais: Just over an hour from Disneyland Paris by train, Beauvais is known for its beautiful Gothic cathedral, which is considered one of the most impressive in all of France. The city also offers a charming medieval old town, a 19th-century market hall and a variety of local restaurants and cafes.

7. Château de Vaux-le-Vicomte: Located about an hour's drive from Disneyland Paris, the Château de Vaux-le-Vicomte is a beautiful 17th-century palace that inspired the design of the Palace of Versailles. The palace is surrounded by stunning gardens, including a French-style formal garden, an English-style garden, and a forested area.

Overall, there are plenty of attractions and places to visit both within and beyond Disneyland Paris, and visitors are sure to find something that interests them.

From the historic cities to the beautiful surrounding countryside, there is no shortage of cultural sites or experiences to enjoy while staying near the 'Happiest Place on Earth'.

Resources and Further Reading

While I hope that this guide has provided you with a wealth of information and insights, there are always more resources and reading materials out there to further enhance your knowledge and enjoyment of the happiest place on Earth.

1. "The Imagineering Field Guide to Disneyland Paris" by Imagineers. This comprehensive guide is like having your very own backstage pass to Disneyland Paris. Packed with insider information and behind-the-scenes stories, it offers a fascinating glimpse into the magic behind the park's creation. From concept art to ride details, this book is a treasure trove for Disney enthusiasts.

2. "Disneyland Paris: From Sketch to Reality" by Imagineers. If you've ever wondered how the magical world of Disneyland Paris came to be, this book is a must-read. Filled with concept art, blueprints, and interviews with the creative minds behind the park, it provides a captivating journey through the evolution of

Disneyland Paris.

3. "The Hidden Mickeys of Disneyland Paris" by Steve Barrett. If you're a fan of the famous Hidden Mickeys scattered throughout the Disney parks, then this book is for you. Uncover the secrets and hidden surprises of Disneyland Paris with this delightful guide. From subtle nods to Disney characters to hidden symbols, you'll never look at the park the same way again.

4. "Disney's Land: Walt Disney and the Invention of the Amusement Park That Changed the World" by Richard Snow. While this book doesn't specifically focus on Disneyland Paris, it offers a captivating account of Walt Disney's vision and the birth of Disneyland in California. By delving into the history and innovations that shaped the Disney parks, you'll gain a deeper appreciation for the magic that awaits you in Disneyland Paris.

5. "Disneyland Paris: The Ultimate Insider's Guide" by Sebastian Rottmair. As the name suggests, this guidebook is your ultimate companion for navigating Disneyland Paris like a pro. With detailed maps, attraction descriptions, and tips for making the most of your visit, it's a valuable resource for first-timers and seasoned Disney fans alike. Plus, the author's witty commentary adds an extra dose of fun to your planning process.

In addition to these recommended resources, don't forget to check out the official Disneyland Paris website for the latest updates, park maps, and special offers. You can also join online Disney fan communities and forums to connect with fellow enthusiasts and exchange tips and advice.

Remember, the key to a memorable Disneyland Paris experience is preparation and a sense of adventure. By arming yourself with knowledge from these resources and immersing yourself in the magic of Disney, you'll be well-equipped to create lifelong memories in the enchanted kingdom. So go forth, explore, and let the magic begin!

Last but not least, I want to express my gratitude to the readers who have embarked on this literary journey with me. Your enthusiasm and support are what keep authors like me motivated to continue writing. Your feedback and reviews will always be cherished, as they provide the fuel to keep improving and creating meaningful content.

Happy reading and magical adventures at Disneyland Paris!

Ebook, Paperback and Hardback cover images are copyright of the Author.

ABOUT THE AUTHOR

Asaf Iqbal

was born in Marston Green, and currently resides in Shropshire. Although he began writing years ago, 2023 marks the year he is finally releasing his books to the world. A father and a grandfather, he enjoys watching movies and TV shows, collecting movie and TV show props, autographs, and staying fit. He also loves traveling, which has inspired his writing.

Asaf is currently working on multiple writing projects spanning various genres, including fantasy, children's books.

He is set to release number of fiction books in 2023. His large family of nine has been an inspiration for his writing, and his preferred themes include Children's moral stories, educational, time travel, alternate dimensions, vampires, supernatural elements, historical events, and lost treasures.

Whether you're a fan of horror or fantasy, Asaf's books are sure to leave you spellbound. So sit back, grab a cup of coffee, and prepare to be transported to a world of dark magic and otherworldly creatures.

Asaf is an avid reader with a collection of 3000 books, and his favourite authors include James Patterson, Clive Cussler, Jonathan Stroud, Stephen King, Gregg Hurwitz, Dan Brown, and David Balacci, Scott Mariani to name a few.

His website, can be found at: https://www.aiqbalauthor.com (Coming Soon) and will feature a blog where he'll share updates on his book series, new releases, favourite reads and connect with his loyal readers.

BOOKS BY THIS AUTHOR

5 Businesses To Start From Home : From Home To Success: Empowering Entrepreneurs With 5 Lucrative Business Ideas

Are you tired of the daily grind and yearning for a more flexible and fulfilling work life?

Look no further!

5 Businesses To Start From Home is your guide to unleashing your entrepreneurial spirit from the comfort of your own home.

This comprehensive book takes you on a journey of exploration, presenting five proven and lucrative business ideas that can be successfully operated without ever leaving your doorstep.

From online ventures to service-based enterprises, each chapter delves into the practical steps, strategies, and tools you need to start and grow your own thriving home-based business.

Discover the freedom, autonomy, and financial potential that awaits you as you embark on this exciting path. Whether you're a stay-at-home parent, a budding entrepreneur, or simply seeking additional income streams, this book empowers you to turn your dreams into reality.

Take charge of your future and unlock the boundless possibilities of home-based entrepreneurship today!

The Correct Mindset To Start A Home Based Business

This book reveals the key principles for cultivating the right mindset to overcome obstacles, develop resilience, and tap into your full potential. Unleash the entrepreneur within and embark on a journey of growth, productivity, and fulfillment as you build your thriving home-based business.

Whether you're a budding entrepreneur seeking the confidence to take the leap or an established business owner looking to recalibrate your mindset, this book serves as a trusted guide to foster the right mental framework for home-based business success.

Are you ready to unlock the keys to success from within? Let this book be your companion as you embark on a transformative quest to build a thriving home-based business.

Autograph Collecting: A Beginners Guide

In "A Beginner's Guide to Autograph Collecting," you can embark on a journey to explore this fascinating world and learn the ropes of building your own autograph collection. Whether you're a seasoned collector or just starting out, this book is packed with valuable insights, practical tips, and expert advice to help you navigate the intricacies of autograph collecting.

Discover the significance of autographs as unique personal possessions and their broader cultural and historical importance. Learn about the different methods of obtaining autographs, including in-person encounters, through the mail, auctions, and estate sales. Explore the thrill of hunting down rare autographs and discover the potential for investment in this captivating hobby.

Authenticity is key when it comes to autograph collecting, and this book will provide you with valuable insights into the authentication process. Uncover advanced techniques and strategies for long-term collection building, ensuring the preservation and value of your prized autographs.

Whether you're captivated by the historical significance, the thrill of the hunt, or the personal connection to your favorite personalities, this guide is your passport to creating a collection that will be cherished for generations to come.

Start your autograph collecting journey today and unlock a world of extraordinary possibilities.

A Guide To Mastering Household Bills & Finances: 2023 Edition

This book was written to help individuals and families reclaim control over their finances and navigate the often overwhelming world of budgeting and saving.

From reducing household bills to maximising government assistance programs, this book equips readers with the tools they need to make informed financial decisions and create lasting positive change in their lives.

If you're ready to take charge of your financial well-being and unlock a world of possibilities.

Get ready to transform your financial outlook, one decision at a time.

Rise And Lift: A Contemporary Approach To Weight Training

Unleash Your Strength. Ignite Your Potential.

In Rise and Lift: A Contemporary Approach to Weight Training, discover a dynamic and transformative guide that takes you on a modern journey into the world of weightlifting. From beginners seeking a fresh start to fitness enthusiasts craving a new perspective, this book empowers you to embark on a lifting journey that will reshape your body, mind, and life.

Step-by-step, you'll master the fundamental principles of weightlifting, uncovering the secrets of proper form, technique, and safety. Dive into the depths of progressive overload and learn how to unlock your body's hidden strength. With an array of lifting techniques, innovative training programs, and comprehensive guidance on nutrition and recovery, you'll find yourself equipped with all the tools needed to sculpt a powerful physique.

But it's not just about physical gains. 'Rise and Lift' recognizes the intrinsic connection between mental and physical well-being. Uncover the mindset and motivation required to overcome obstacles, stay consistent, and achieve lasting results. Immerse yourself in inspiring real-life stories of transformation, and let them fuel your determination to rise above limitations.

Whether you seek to build strength, sculpt muscles, or enhance your overall fitness, Rise and Lift presents a contemporary approach that caters to all ages and genders. Prepare to witness your body and spirit soar to new heights as you embrace weightlifting as a transformative path to unleash your true potential.

Get ready to rise above. Get ready to lift.